"Our Pal God"
and Other Presumptions

"OUR PAL GOD"
and Other Presumptions

A Book of Jewish Humor

JEFFRY V. MALLOW

iUniverse Star
New York Lincoln Shanghai

"OUR PAL GOD" and Other Presumptions
A Book of Jewish Humor

Copyright © 2005, 2008 by Jeffry V. Mallow

All rights reserved. No part of this book may be used or reproduced by any means, graphic, electronic, or mechanical, including photocopying, recording, taping or by any information storage retrieval system without the written permission of the publisher except in the case of brief quotations embodied in critical articles and reviews.

iUniverse Star
an iUniverse, Inc. imprint

iUniverse books may be ordered through booksellers or by contacting:

iUniverse
2021 Pine Lake Road, Suite 100
Lincoln, NE 68512
www.iuniverse.com
1-800-Authors (1-800-288-4677)

Because of the dynamic nature of the Internet, any Web addresses or links contained in this book may have changed since publication and may no longer be valid.

The views expressed in this work are solely those of the author and do not necessarily reflect the views of the publisher, and the publisher hereby disclaims any responsibility for them.

ISBN: 978-1-58348-628-3 (pbk)
ISBN: 978-0-595-90426-6 (ebk)

Printed in the United States of America

CONTENTS

Introduction 1

Part One   *Laughing Inward*

Really Old Jokes 9
Matchmakers 10
Rabbis and Rebbes 13
Cantors 17
Circumcisers 18
Jews and Booze 20
Holy Days 21
Chelmites 25
Rich and Poor 27
Death 31
Internecine Humor 35
Logic I: Talmudic Reasoning 40
Logic II: Goyisher Kop, Yiddisher Kop 42
Logic III: This You Call Logic? 48
Heretics, Atheists, Freethinkers, Converts 50
Small Business, Big Business—Waiters, Seamstresses, Tailors,
   Cabbies, and Other Entrepreneurs 57

Our Pal, God. 65
Zionism and Israel. 68
Sex. 75
Family 80

Part Two   *Laughing Outward*

European Jewish Humor 89
Disputations 90
Czarist Russia 92
Western Europe. 96
Nazis 98
The Soviet Union 101
Poland. 104
American Jewish Humor 106
Immigrants 107
Patriots 108
Education 110
Sports 112
Alrightniks and Show-Offs 114
A New Type, Made in USA. 115
Dialogue I: Jews and Gentiles 116
Dialogue II: Priests, Ministers, and Rabbis. 118
Gentiles: Such Puzzling Folk 121
Popery. 122

Part Three   *Language Humor, Mainly Yiddish*
Pure Yiddish Jokes 127
Language Contact Jokes 130
Bilingual and Multilingual Jokes 138
Jokes that Do, Almost Do, and Do Not Translate. 145

Part Four   *None of the Above*
Compare and Contrast—Jewish/Non-Jewish Variants 155
Chutzpah 172
Out-of-This-World Humor 176

The Future?. 179
Glossary 181

INTRODUCTION

Many years ago, in what was an otherwise relatively humorless existence as a doctoral student in physics, I began collecting Jewish jokes. It started simply. I heard a joke, retold it, and exchanged jokes with friends. I then began collecting books of Jewish humor—first in Yiddish and then in other languages as well. As my collection grew, a kind of growth principle took over, like a runaway nuclear chain reaction. For every joke I told, I acquired at least two new ones in exchange. In short order, the thing was completely out of hand. I took to carrying blank scraps of paper to Jewish events in case I heard new jokes. In extreme cases, I wrote them down on the napkins. (Jewish events always include food, and physicists are adept at napkin-writing.)

I began doing stand-up comedy. Sometimes, it was in the guise of a lecture on Jewish humor; other times, it was club dates with Chicago's Maxwell Street Klezmer Band. Of course, in these situations, when the audience was larger than what would fit in someone's living room, so was the ratio of new jokes acquired per old joke told. I was forced to computerize. This book is the result.

Many books are written about the meaning and purpose(s) of humor. Some have focused on Jewish humor. I'm not going to repeat the insights of others, but I'd like to share some of my own with you. Here, for example, are some of the rules I've learned about Jewish humor and humor in general:

- **Rule One:** There are (almost) no new jokes. For nearly any joke I hear or read, I either know it already from somewhere else or it will crop up later in some variation or other. The locales of the stories are separated by thousands of miles and hundreds—sometimes thousands—of years, but the basic jokes are the same. When the variations are interesting, I'll give you both—or several—versions.

- **Rule Two:** Rule One is not exactly true. Some Jewish jokes are very specific to a locale. For example, I'll tell you some American Jewish jokes and some French Jewish jokes. Neither of which, like their respective wines, travel well.

- **Rule Three:** There are variants of what we think of as Jewish jokes in other cultures. (Note that I'm using "culture" in the broadest sense. Some Jewish jokes reappear as Irish jokes, scientist jokes, nonspecific jokes coming over the

Internet, and so forth.) Sometimes the humor is identical; sometimes the particular culture gives the joke a unique spin. I'll give you these variants, too.

- **Rule Four:** Rule Three is not exactly true. I think there is one area in which Jewish humor is unique: language humor. It isn't that there aren't any Irish jokes about Erse or Mexican jokes about Spanish. (There are.) However, Jews have encountered many cultures and languages while speaking their own unique tongues. This has had a profound—and delightful—effect on language-based jokes. I have devoted a section of this book to such jokes. Don't worry! You do not have to speak any language except English to understand these jokes because I will explain them. However, as we all know, jokes that are explained don't seem that funny.

- **Rule Five:** Timing is everything ... or nearly so. Jokes are usually meant to be told, not read. I envy humor columnists because I think they accomplish an almost insurmountable task. Personally, I'd prefer to be in your living room right now instead of having you read this book. But trust me, these jokes have all been field-tested on audiences of the toughest sort, my fellow Jews. The opening story in Immanuel Olsvanger's collection of Yiddish jokes, *Royte Pomerantsn*, goes like this:

  > Tell a peasant a joke, he laughs three times: when he hears it, when you explain it, and when he finally gets it. Tell an officer a joke, he laughs twice: when he hears it and when you explain it—because he'll never get it. Tell a landowner a joke, and he laughs once: when he hears it. He'll never get it, and he won't let you explain it. Tell a Jew a joke, and he interrupts you with the remark, "Feh, an old story!" Then he tells it better!

  I am grateful to all of those audience members who have improved on my jokes. Conversely, I have always taken the liberty of trying to improve on stories I have heard—as does anyone who tells jokes. That's why—as you will see—there are numerous variants of a single story.

- **Rule Six:** Categories are artificial constructs. But people like patterns, and books must have some order. So, I have divided the jokes into different groupings, according to some organizing principle (and even I am not sure what it is). Don't take it too seriously. If you think some jokes belong in other categories, all I can say, quoting the rabbi adjudicating between two disputants, is, "You're right. And you're also right."

You will find quite a few terms in Yiddish, Hebrew, and some other languages throughout the book. Don't worry. The first time such a term appears, I will footnote it at the bottom of the same page, *azoy*.[1] Useful terms or terms used more than once will also be listed and elaborated on in the Glossary at the end of the book. (You should definitely look at the Glossary. It might amuse you.) However, the phrases specific to a particular joke appear only once, as footnotes on the page where the joke itself appears.

A word about the spelling of Yiddish words in English. I will mostly use the orthography standardized by the YIVO (Yiddisher Visnshaftlekher Institut) Institute for Jewish Research, the preeminent institution devoted to the study of Yiddish and East European Jewish culture. For our purposes, this means the following:

- *kh* represents the guttural as in "Yekh!"
- *ay* represents the vowel sound as in "Aye, aye, sir!"
- *ey* represents the vowel sound as in "Hey!"
- *o* represents the vowel sound as in "love."
- *i* represents the vowel sound as in "it" or "elite," but not as in "ivory."
- *e* at the end of a word is pronounced as "Eh."

In addition, when Yiddish has consonants clustered together with no vowel sound *e* between them, no vowel is written. (The technical term is *shewa*.) For example, *shatkhn* is a matchmaker. We have the *shewa* in English, too. We don't pronounce the *e* in *oven*, do we? We could spell it *ovn*.

Only in those cases in which a spelling has become familiar in English will I diverge from YIVO orthography. For example, egg twist bread will be written "challah" (like at the bakery), not *khale* (like at YIVO). "Pray" will be rendered as "daven" instead of *davn*, which is how it's really pronounced. "Luck" will be written "mazel," not *mazl*. In the Glossary, I will list the popular spelling. The YIVO standard orthography will follow in parentheses.

What kinds of stories will you *not* find in this book? While I have included many jokes in which Jews mock their oppressors and themselves, you will not find any nasty racist humor here, either about Jews or by Jews. A school of thought claims ethnic jokes are a healthy outlet for negative feelings about other groups. I do not believe this to be so. I think those jokes tend to reinforce negative stereotypes, so I don't tell them. For example, you will find a few gentle jokes Jews tell about their own reputed cleverness in business, but none of the mean-

---

1. Like this

spirited stories overt or covert anti-Semites tell. Nor am I a big fan of goyisher kop[2] humor, which mocks the purported stupidity of Gentiles. (I will discuss this further in the Goyisher Kop, Yiddisher Kop section.[3]) This is not to say there isn't something funny about these types of stories. However, I think of them as the comic equivalent of the anti-Semitic poetry of T. S. Eliot and Ezra Pound. Are those "bad" poems? Not at all. They are good because they resonate—unfortunately—with feelings of the people who read them. But who needs it? My mother, of blessed memory, would say, "Es past nisht" (It's unbecoming).

Are there, however, some stories that are okay if a member of the group itself tells it, but not okay if an outsider tells it? I think so. Here's one:

> Six-year-old Patrick O'Connor invites his friend, Maurie Cohen, to sit in on his Sunday school class. The teacher, a nun, offers the children twenty-five cents if they can tell her who the most important person in the Bible is. Maurie's hand shoots up, and he answers, without hesitation, "Jesus."
>
> "You're right," says the sister, handing him his reward. "But I'm surprised someone of the Jewish faith would realize this."
>
> "Listen," says Maurie, "it's really Moses, but business is business."

Told by a Jew, the underlying message is a reinforcement of cultural beliefs that: (1) we live by our wits, and (2) when you're a minority dealing with the majority, you sometimes have to go along to get along. Told by a Gentile, the message is more likely to be, "Jews will do anything for money."

What do Jews laugh at? Almost anything is fair game. A more pertinent question is perhaps, "Who do Jews laugh at?" The answer is inward (at ourselves and each other) and outward (at "the other"). That is, we laugh at our own foibles as a community. Targets range from rabbis to cantors to matchmakers, and from the overly pious to the freethinkers and heretics. We laugh at each other: Ashkenazim[4] at Sephardim,[5] Yeckes[6] at Ostjuden,[7] Litvaks[8] at Galitsianers,[9] and vice

---

2. Gentile head
3. Jewish head
4. European Jews
5. Jews from Arab countries; originally Jews from the Iberian Peninsula; expelled in the fifteenth century
6. German Jews
7. East European Jews
8. Lithuanian Jews
9. Jews from the Galicia region of southeastern Poland

versa. Finally, we laugh at our non-Jewish oppressors. Humor is a potent weapon for survival in difficult and often desperate circumstances.

Jewish humor dates back at least to the Bible. It is liberally sprinkled throughout the Talmud.[10] Many jokes span both time and space, retaining their pungency century after century and in places as far apart as Eastern Europe, America, North Africa, and Israel. Other tales are specific constructions for new places and new times or for the transitions from one country or epoch to another. Some Jewish humor is not even specifically Jewish. Other peoples have the same jokes in their own variants. Some Jewish humor varies from one Jewish community to another to fit specific circumstances. We will see examples of all of these.

Variants of many of the jokes in this collection can be found in other compilations in various languages, although they are not categorized in the same way. Some I have consulted are Nathan Ausubel's *A Treasury of Jewish Humor*, Elie Baroukh and David Lemberg's *5000 ans d'humour juif*, Danish Forlaget Micro's *Humørpiller*, Marc Hillel's *Israël: 30 ans d'humour*, William Novak and Moshe Waldoks's *Big Book of Jewish Humor*, Marc-Alain Ouaknin and Dory Rotnemer's two-volume *La bible de l'humour juif*, Immanuel Olsvanger's *Royte Pomerantsn* and *L'Chaim*, J. Ch. Rabnitski's *Yiddishe Vitsn*, Henry Spalding's *Encyclopedia of Jewish Humor* and *Joys of Jewish Humor*, and Rabbi Joseph Telushkin's *Jewish Humor: What the Best Jokes Say About the Jews*. My primary consultants, however, have been the hundreds of people who come up to me at one of my gigs and say, "Have I got one for you." My thanks to all of them.

---

10. The great codex of Jewish law

PART ONE
LAUGHING INWARD

We begin with humor directed inward, at the Jewish people themselves.

REALLY OLD JOKES

It would be impossible to say what the oldest Jewish joke is, but the Ten Commandments is probably the oldest Jewish joke theme.

> After smashing the first set of tablets, Moses returns with the second set.
> "I have good news and bad news," he announces to the assembled Israelites. "The good news is: I got him down to only ten. The bad news is: adultery stays in."

A variant once appeared as a cartoon:

> Among the assembled Israelites listening to Moses read the Ten Commandments are a man and a woman. He says to her, "If this is retroactive to last Thursday, we're in big trouble!"

MATCHMAKERS

Persisting throughout the centuries of Jewish life, one of the great themes of Jewish humor is matchmaking. It continues even now, when the custom has presumably fallen out of fashion, except among the extreme Orthodox. (I say presumably because the many personal ads in magazines are simply a newer version of the old custom.) The theme of the humor is simple. A shatkhn[1] will do anything to convince the prospective partners to make the match. Traditionally, the bride's qualities had to be presented to the groom and his family; thus, most stories start with that scenario.

> A shatkhn comes to a prospective groom and announces, "Have I got a match for you!"
>
> The young man, no great match himself: homely, not too bright, and a bit egocentric, says, "So let's hear."
>
> "She has all the virtues," says the shatkhn. "She is beautiful, clever, well-educated, and from a wealthy family. But I won't lie to you. She has one flaw. One hour out of every year, she is completely meshuge."[2]
>
> "That's not a problem," says the young man. "I can live with that. Call her and make the match."
>
> "Not so fast," says the shatkhn. "With such a groom as you, I have to wait for that hour to ask her."

A slightly different version:

> A not-very-attractive prospective groom says to the shatkhn, "I know Rokhl Cohen is looking for a husband. She is quite clever, good-looking, and well-educated. Why don't you propose a match between her and me?"
>
> The shatkhn replies, "Frankly, she would have to be meshuge to marry you."

---

1. Matchmaker
2. Crazy. (Don't forget to pronounce the *e* at the end of these words!)

"Okay," says the young man, "I can live with meshuge."

A shatkhn comes to a prospective groom and announces, "Have I got a match for you! Reyzl Levy is charming, intelligent, from a good family."

"But," complains the groom, "she has an awful limp."

"Only when she walks," replies the shatkhn.

A shatkhn is training his new assistant. "Whatever I say, you exaggerate it." They approach the family of the prospective groom. The shatkhn says, "Have I got a bride for you."

The assistant adds, "A bride? A bride with virtues the likes of which no one has ever seen!"

The shatkhn says, "She's very pretty."

The assistant adds, "Pretty? Beautiful like the moon and stars!"

"And clever," says the shatkhn,

"Clever? A real Einstein!" says the assistant.

"Also quite well-off," says the shatkhn.

"Well-off? Like Rothschild!" says the assistant.

"However," says the shatkhn, "she does have a small hump on her back."

"Hump?" says the assistant. "A veritable mountain!"

A shatkhn comes to a prospective groom and announces, "Have I got a match for you! She's pretty, clever, from a good family. They have invited you to dinner this Shabbes."[3]

The young man, a bit shy, asks, "But what will I talk to her about?"

The shatkhn replies, "You can surely talk to her about three things: family, love, and philosophy."

The young man memorizes this sage counsel and goes off to the Shabbes dinner. Seated next to his potential spouse, he asks her, "Do you have a brother?"

"No," she replies. End of family discussion.

The soup is served. He asks her, "Don't you just love cabbage soup?"

"No," she replies. End of love discussion. He's down to his last card—philosophy.

"If you had a brother, would he love cabbage soup?"

---

3.   Sabbath

A shatkhn comes to a prospective groom and announces, "Have I got a match for you! She's pretty, well-educated, and from a wealthy and aristocratic family."

The young man and his parents, all of whom have an excessively positive view of his limited virtues, ask, "So who is it?"

"The Princess of Denmark," replies the shatkhn.

"A shikse?[4] Not for our boy!"

But the shatkhn eventually convinces them it's a good match. Maybe she'll convert, who knows? So they sign the contract. The shatkhn exits to the street, mops his brow, and mutters, "Well, that's half the battle."

A shatkhn comes to a prospective groom and announces, "Have I got a match for you! She's as beautiful as a work of art!"

The young man agrees to meet the prospect. When the shatkhn returns a few days later, the young man is furious.

"A work of art? Some work of art! One eye half-closed! The other too large. One ear a good inch below the other, and the nose off-center by at least a half-inch!"

"So," asks the shatkhn, "Picasso you don't like?"

In France, a shatkhn comes to a prospective groom and announces, "Have I got a match for you! It's Rachelle Birnboym."

The young man replies, "She seems very nice, but the only problem is she's like the Dreyfus Affair."

"What do you mean, like the Dreyfus Affair?" asks the puzzled shatkhn.

"Well," says the young man, "she protests her innocence, but the officers of the mess claim otherwise."

---

4. Gentile girl or woman; sometimes pejorative

RABBIS AND REBBES

Of course, rabbis and their Hassidic[1] counterparts, rebbes, are the focus of many stories. The themes vary. Throughout most, however, the notion is that Jews render their rabbis either too much respect ... or too little.

> A Hassid[2] decides he will make a pilgrimage to the great rebbe of Smilovsk and learn wisdom at his feet. After an arduous journey of many weeks, the Hassid arrives at the court of the rebbe, just as the sage is explaining the meaning of life to his followers.
> "Life," says the rebbe, "is like a dish of strawberries."
> The followers nod wisely. The newly arrived Hassid, however, asks, "Rebbe, how is life like a dish of strawberries?"
> The rebbe ponders the question for some time and replies, "You mean, life *isn't* like a dish of strawberries?"

A variant:

> The rebbe says, "Life is like a dish of strawberries."
> The Hassid asks, "How is life like a dish of strawberries?"
> "How should I know?" asks the rebbe. "What am I, a philosopher?"

Woody Allen tells a related tale. It is funny because it is so ridiculous:

> A Hassid asks his rebbe, "Rebbe, why are we Jews enjoined from eating pork?"
> The rebbe replies, "No pork? Uh-oh!"

---

1. Hassidic, the adjective for a follower of Hassidism, a branch of Judaism founded by Israel Baal Shem Tov in the eighteenth century. Hassidism is given to religious ecstasy. While not antischolastic, it was a reaction against an overintellectualized Judaism that honored the scholar to the exclusion of simple, pious folk.
2. A male follower of Hassidism. Actual Yiddish pronunciation is KHO-sed. A female follower is a *khside*, pronounced kh-SEE-deh. The plurals are *khsidim* and *khsides*, respectively.

On the other hand, there's the story of the woman who comes to the rabbi with a question about a soup she is making. It's a beef soup, and her little son's hat has fallen into it. Is the soup still kosher?[3]
"What was on the hat?" asks the rabbi.
"Well, you know how little boys are. My son was playing in the mud, on the road where all the animals are taken to market. You can imagine what kind of dirt was on the hat."
"That's not a problem," says the rabbi. "What else?"
"He had hair lice last week, and I think one of the parts of a dead louse was on the hat."
"No problem," says the rabbi. "Anything else?"
"He fell and cut his forehead, and I think his scab came off onto the hat."
"Still seems all right. Is that all?"
"Well," replies the mother, "I had put some butter on the scab to soften it ..."
"Treyf!"[4] shouts the rabbi.

After giving his very first sermon, the new rabbi comes very concerned to the synagogue president.
"Mr. Levy just told me my sermon was the worst he's ever heard."
"Oh, don't worry about Levy," the president reassures the rabbi. "That fool always blurts out what everyone's thinking."

A father brings his young son to the rabbi of the synagogue.
"My boy thinks he'd like to be a rabbi. Can you answer some questions he has?"
"Certainly," says the rabbi. "Ask away, young man."
The lad replies, "Just what is it a rabbi does every day? It seems all you have to do is pray for a few minutes and then give a sermon on Friday."
"Young fellow," says the rabbi, "you don't want to be a rabbi. You are destined to become a synagogue president."

A Reform synagogue hires its first female rabbi. Eager to impress the congregation, she prepares brilliant sermons and delivers them eloquently every Friday night for six months. During each sermon, she glances over to the synagogue president, only to find him fast asleep. Finally, she can't stand it.

---

3. In keeping with Jewish law regarding food. The strictures include no meat and milk products eaten together. No shellfish. No pork. Definitely no bacon cheeseburgers.
4. Nonkosher

"I assume you do not find me adequate because you sleep through all my sermons."

"On the contrary," protests the president, "it shows how much confidence I have in you."

A Jewish peddler finds himself in a strange shtetl[5] as the sun is setting one Friday afternoon. He hurries over to the synagogue before Shabbes and asks the rabbi to put his money into safekeeping until Saturday evening. The worthy agrees and locks it in the desk of his study. After spending a pleasant Shabbes in the town, the peddler comes to the rabbi and asks for his money. "What money?" asks the rabbi. "I don't have any of your money."

"But five of your congregants saw me give you the money!"

"Let's ask them," says the rabbi.

He calls the five witnesses. Each swears the peddler never gave the rabbi anything. The poor man, completely dejected, begins making his way out of the town and home. Suddenly, he sees the rabbi approaching him with a bag, in which is all of his money.

"Here's your money," says the rabbi.

"But why did you deny having it and then get five of your congregants to support you?" asks the bewildered peddler.

The rabbi sighs. "I just wanted to show a fellow Jew what scoundrels I have to put up with in this miserable shtetl."

An elderly Orthodox and a young Reform rabbi decide to hold a joint assembly in which they will try to answer any question posed by the community.

One fellow raises his hand and asks, "If I think that I don't think, am I thinking, or am I not thinking?"

The Orthodox rabbi shakes his head back and forth and asks the man to repeat the question. He does. The rabbi again shakes his head back and forth and asks again for a repetition of the question.

"What's the matter?" asks his Reform colleague. "Why can't you understand the question?"

The Orthodox rabbi looks plaintively at his colleague, "Why can't he talk with his hands?"

In honor of his twenty-fifth year of service, a rabbi receives an all-expenses paid trip to Miami from his congregation. When he checks into his suite at the Hotel Fontainbleau, he discovers a beautiful woman, naked on the bed.

---

5. Eastern European Jewish village

"What are you doing here?" he asks.

"I'm part of the congregation's gift to you. They wanted it to be a surprise."

The rabbi stalks over to the phone, places a call to the president of the synagogue, and proceeds to berate him. "How could you do such a thing? I'm shocked and appalled!" And he slams down the phone.

He turns around to see the woman getting dressed. "Where are you going?" says the rabbi. "I'm not mad at you."

CANTORS

Cantors certainly come in for their share of jibes. Traditionally, they were the leaders of public prayer, the pillars of the synagogue service. As such, they reputedly began putting on airs. This stereotype, coupled with another that suggests a good voice doesn't necessarily denote a good brain, led to many jokes at the cantor's expense. The archetypical one is the following:

> The rabbi, the cantor, and the shammes[1] are preparing the synagogue for the upcoming High Holy Days. The rabbi, overcome with piety, suddenly drops on his face in front of the Ark of the Torah[2] and shouts, "Lord, in thine eyes, I am nothing!"
> The cantor, not to be outdone, drops on his face and shouts, "Lord, in thine eyes, I am nothing!"
> The shammes quickly follows suit, "Lord, in thine eyes, I am nothing!"
> The cantor turns over on his side and mutters to the rabbi, "Look who thinks he's nothing."

That's it? One cantor joke? No, but the others are found in the section on Language Humor.

---

1. Beadle, caretaker. Pronounced SHAH-mess
2. Literally, the scroll containing the first five books of the Bible, as in this joke. However, it can also refer to the entire body of Jewish knowledge.

CIRCUMCISERS

One more figure in Jewish life is the source of a great deal of humor—the moyhel.[1] Are any of these jokes tasteless? Need you ask?

> A fellow is visiting a strange town when he notices his watch has stopped. He walks down the main street and comes upon a storefront filled with watches in display cases, in the windows, and on the walls. He walks in and asks the proprietor to repair his watch.
> "I don't fix watches. I'm a moyhel," is the reply.
> "Then why do you have watches displayed everywhere?" asks the frustrated customer.
> The proprietor replies, "So what would you like me to display?"

> Two chaps are at adjacent urinals in a public washroom. One says to the other, "You're Jewish, aren't you?"
> "Yes," the second man replies.
> "And from St. Louis," continues the first.
> "Amazing! You're right!"
> "And you were born between 1946 and 1956, yes?"
> "Yes!"
> "And your bris[2] was performed by Moyhel Cohen?"
> "Absolutely! How do you know?"
> "Simple," comes the reply, "He always cut on a bias. You're peeing on my shoes."

> A moyhel retires after sixty years of cutting-edge service to his community. Disgustingly enough, he has saved all his tips and decides to leave a legacy for his grandson. He takes the huge box of foreskins to the local leather maker and asks him to make something out of them.
> "Come back next week. It'll be done."

---

1. Ritual circumciser
2. Circumcision; performed eight days after birth. *Bris* means literally "covenant," denoting the contract between the Jews and God.

The moyhel returns the next week and is handed a nicely crafted wallet.

"That's it?" he asks with disappointment. "From all that material, just one wallet?"

"Yeah," says the leather maker, "but, when you rub it, it turns into a suitcase."

JEWS AND BOOZE

This is going to be a very short section. It's well known Jews have a very low rate of alcoholism, whether due to genetics, culture, or both. (You'll find one Jewish drunk story in the Logic I: Talmudic Reasoning section.) Only in Jewish restaurants does the waiter's question, "Red or white?" refer to horseradish.

Jews usually ascribe the cause of their sobriety to the quality of the beverage and/or the circumstances in which it is imbibed. The first experience of every Jewish male with wine, eight days after birth (see the previous section), is accompanied by such unpleasantness that it probably has a lifelong aversive effect. In any case, we always drink with our legs crossed.

As for the quality of Jewish wine, the vintage is less likely to be described as "1993" than as "last Tuesday." In addition, drunkenness is almost impossible because it is preceded by insulin shock.

So here's a riddle:

> Why are French wines stored on their sides while Jewish wines are stored upright?
> With French wine, you don't want the cork to dry out. With Jewish wine, you don't want the bottle cap to rust.

HOLY DAYS

Jewish holy days—from the Shabbes to Rosh Hashonah,[1] Yom Kippur,[2] and Pesakh[3]—are not immune from Jewish wit.

> A synagogue is deeply divided over a question of ritual and tradition. Does the congregation recite the Shma[4] sitting or standing? Half the congregants do it one way; the other half do it the other way. Throughout the solemn prayer, they shout at each other, "Stand up!" "No, you sit down!"
> Finally, the rancor becomes too much, and they decide to consult one of the founders of the congregation. They call him at his senior citizens' condo in Miami and ask, "Was the tradition for the congregation to stand while reciting the Shma?"
> He thinks and replies, "No, that wasn't it."
> "Well, was the tradition for the congregation to sit while reciting the Shma?"
> He searches his memory. "No, that wasn't it either."
> "But how can that be? Right now, we have half the congregation standing, the other half sitting, and everyone is yelling at everyone else."
> "Ah," says the elder, "That was the tradition!"

It is required that Jews who have been quarreling with each other make peace before Yom Kippur. Asking and receiving forgiveness from one's fellow must precede asking forgiveness from God.

> Two Jews who have been at each others' throats for the entire year are persuaded to meet and reconcile.

---

1. Jewish New Year; occurs in the fall
2. Day of Atonement; eight days after Rosh Hashonah
3. Passover; springtime festival celebrating Moses having led the Jews out of slavery in Egypt
4. The fundamental credo of Jewish monotheism. It begins, "Shma yisroel adonoy eloheynu, adonoy ekhod (Hear O Israel, the Lord our God, the Lord is One)." "Barukh shem kvod malkhuso leyolam voed (Blessed is His glorious kingdom forever and ever)."

Moishe says, "I forgive you for any wrongs I feel you did me during the year, and I ask for your forgiveness."
Khatskl replies, "I forgive you, and I also ask your forgiveness."
"I forgive you, "says Moishe, "and I wish for you in the coming year all that you wish for me."
"Oh," says Khatskl, "you're starting again already?"

A Jew passes a pet store and sees a sign: "Davening Parrot." A parrot that can daven?[5] This he's got to see. He goes in and asks to hear the bird daven. The proprietor says to the parrot, "Daven the Rosh Hashonah service." With that, the parrot reaches under one wing, whips out a yarmulke,[6] reaches under the other, whips out a siddur,[7] and begins to daven the service. Flawlessly.
The Jew says, "I'll buy him."
One month later is Rosh Hashonah. The Jew brings the parrot to the service and starts laying bets. Ten to one the parrot can daven the service. When all the pledges are down (without real money being exchanged—after all, it is Rosh Hashonah!), he says to the parrot, "Daven."
No response. The parrot sits there, silent. The owner is humiliated and in serious debt. He stalks out of the synagogue with the parrot. After they're out of earshot, he demands, "Why didn't you daven? I know you can do it! You just cost me a pile of dough!"
"Relax," says the parrot. "We're gonna clean up on Yom Kippur."

For some reason, there is a thriving industry of Jewish animal jokes. Here are two more:
A man walks into synagogue with a dog. The shammes comes up to him and says, "No dogs allowed."
The man replies, "This is a Jewish dog." The shammes sees the dog has a bag around its neck.
"Rover," says the man, "daven!"
"The dog opens the bag, takes out a yarmulke, a talles,[8] and a siddur and starts to daven.

---

5. Pray; referring only to Jewish prayer service. Note, it's pronounced DAV-n, short *a*, no *e* sound.
6. Skullcap
7. Prayer book
8. Prayer shawl

"That's fantastic," says the shammes. "You should take him to Hollywood. He could make millions!"

"You tell him," says the man. "He wants to be a dentist."

A synagogue has a problem: a family of squirrels living in the building. The Board of Directors votes to have the squirrels caught and released in a local forest preserve. Which they do. Three times. Within forty-eight hours, the squirrel family is back in the synagogue.

Finally, in desperation, the Board votes the squirrels in as members of the synagogue. It works. Now they only turn up on Rosh Hashonah and Yom Kippur.

Mrs. Goldfarb is famous for her homemade Pesakh sponge cake, so famous the local newspaper gets wind of it and sends out a reporter for the recipe.

"First," says Mrs. Goldfarb, "you fry an onion."

"An onion?" asks the astounded reporter.

"Yeh," replies Mrs. Goldfarb. "Why shouldn't the house smell good while you're baking a sponge cake?"

A blind guy at a Seder inadvertently picks up a piece of matzoh[9] instead of the Braille Haggadah,[10] runs his fingers over it, and demands, "Who wrote this crap?"

The Talmud has rules about Pesakh, one of which the rabbi invokes in his pre-Passover sermon.

"Remember," he admonishes the congregation, "do not eat matzoh before Pesakh. To do so, says our Talmud, is as if to make love to your fiancée in her father's parlor."

With which, an elderly male congregant leaps to his feet and shouts, "Rabbi, there's no comparison whatsoever!"

Yom Kippur is a day when the prayer service is not only long, but coupled with fasting.

A young boy is in synagogue when he sees a plaque on the wall with the names of members of the congregation who had been killed fighting in World War II.

---

9. Unleavened bread with ridges and perforations, eaten throughout Passover, to commemorate the tradition that the Jews fleeing Egypt did not have any time to let their bread rise
10. Passover service book

"What's this?" he asks.

"Those are the names of people who died in the service," answers his mother.

"Morning or afternoon?"

CHELMITES

There are many tales of the famous Wise Men of Chelm. This real town in Eastern Europe is a source of legend and humor. An angel carrying a sack of wise souls and a sack of foolish souls supposedly dropped one of them on the town. Which one? Who knows? But the Chelmites have unique explanations for every question and unique solutions for every problem. Here are some examples:

A Jew walking home at night sees a Chelmite searching the ground under a streetlamp.
"Can I help?" asks the newcomer.
"Yes, I lost my keys."
"Do you know approximately where?"
"Yes," replies the Chelmite, "there at the corner of the building."
"But why," asks the other man, "are you looking for them under the streetlamp?"
"Because," replies the Wise Man of Chelm, "here the light is better."

"Which is more important," a Chelmite was once asked, "the moon or the sun?"
"The moon, of course. It shines at night when it's dark. The sun only shines in the day when it's light."

A Wise Man of Chelm watches his wife do the laundry at the river. As she beats out his underwear, he turns his eyes toward heaven and says, "Oh, thank you, Lord, thank you!"
"How nice of you," says a neighbor, "to thank God for giving you such an industrious wife."
"Not at all," replies the Chelmite. "I'm thanking him that I'm not in that underwear."

North African Jews tell a similar tale about their folk hero, Djoha, who is sitting on his balcony when a jalaba[1] his wife has hung out to dry blows off and falls three stories to the street.

> "Thank God," he says.
>
> "For what?" replies his wife angrily. "For bringing a wind to blow your newly washed jalaba into the gutter?"
>
> "No," says Djoha, "for not putting me in the jalaba at the time."

> A woman comes to the Rabbi of Chelm.
>
> "I sent my husband out to buy a challah[2] last Friday. Today is Thursday, and he hasn't returned. What should I do?"
>
> The rabbi ponders the question for a few minutes. Finally, he replies, "I don't think you can count on your husband. Tomorrow, send one of your children for the challah."

---

1. Shiftlike robe worn by both men and women in the Middle East
2. Egg twist bread; eaten on the Sabbath

RICH AND POOR

In Eastern Europe, there was constant struggle between the few rich Jews and the many poor ones. It wasn't that some of the rich weren't charitable, but the Jews took the Hebrew word for charity, *tsedakah*, which connotes something acquired by right, quite seriously. The Jews never thought wealth was a sign of God's grace. Getting rich was just luck, as was remaining poor. Some of the wealthiest Jewish families—Rothschild, Brodsky, De Hirsch—were even the butt of special jokes that named them by name.

> Two Jewish women are walking down the street when they see a beautiful baby carriage, gilt-edged and lined with expensive fur, coming toward them. They ask the nursemaid who the child is.
> "That's the new Brodsky baby," she replies.
> One of the women turns to the other and says with awe, "So young and already Brodsky?"

> Baron de Hirsch was wont to give two beggar brothers fifty zlotys[1] each on Friday afternoon. One Friday, the customary knock on the door comes. The baron opens it to see only one beggar.
> "Where is your brother?"
> The beggar replies, "He passed away earlier this week."
> "I'm terribly sorry to hear it," says De Hirsch, giving the beggar fifty zlotys.
> "But what about my brother's fifty?" asks the beggar.
> "You just told me he was dead," replies the baron.
> "So who's his heir," says the beggar. "You or me?"

> The rabbi approaches a wealthy Jew and asks him for alms for the poor Jews in the shtetl.
> "I'm sorry. I can't give you any money. I have a poor brother and sister," says the rich man. The rabbi leaves empty-handed. Some days later, the rabbi sees two beggars, a man and a woman, at the synagogue. He asks who they are and discovers they are that very brother and sister. He also discovers they get

---

1.   A Polish coin

no help from their rich sibling. The rabbi returns to the rich man's house and confronts him, "What do you mean you can't give me alms for the poor because you have a poor brother and sister? You do nothing for them!"
"Exactly," replies the wealthy man. "If I don't even help my own family, how can you possibly expect me to give money to strangers?"

Just as wealth was not considered a sign of God's favor, neither was it considered a mark of intelligence.

A rich Jew hires a poor melamed [2] to teach his young son the prayers. After a week, the Jew asks the melamed how it's coming.
"Well," says the melamed, "I've been spending the week teaching him the Kaddish."[3]
"What?" exclaims the wealthy Jew. "I'm still young and in good health!"
"Yes," replies the melamed, "but by the time your son masters the Kaddish ..."

A young Jew, an adherent of the radical politics sweeping Eastern Europe in the late nineteenth century, comes to his rabbi and exclaims enthusiastically, "Rabbi, you must help me. We have to convince the Jews of our town that the rich should share their wealth with the poor!"
"I will be happy to help, my son," replies the old rabbi. "Let's divide the labor. I'll convince the poor."

Motl is telling his wife Sheyndl of his recent train ride.
"I was sitting in the carriage, and you won't believe what happened. The conductor came in and looked at me as if I was traveling without a ticket."
"So what did you do?" asks Sheyndl.
"What could I do?" says Motl. "I looked back at him as if I was traveling with a ticket."

A beggar sits on the same street corner every day for five years. Each day, one kind passerby gives him a coin. One day, the passerby, much pained by the beggar's situation, stops and asks, "Have you no family?"
"Yes, indeed," says the beggar. "I have a son who runs a successful business and a daughter who is a well-known attorney."
"So why don't you let them help you?"
"What?" says the beggar. "And lose my independence?"

---

2. Teacher of young children
3. Prayer for a dead parent or other loved one

One night, noises in the pantry awaken Djoha and his wife.
"I think it's a burglar, Djoha. Why don't you go down and surprise him before he steals anything?"
Djoha doesn't move.
"Are you afraid?" asks his wife.
"No, ashamed," replies Djoha. "Our dishes are all cracked, and our silverware is fake."

Mendl, coming out of synagogue, sees a beggar in a yarmulke with his hand out for a contribution.
"Wait a minute," says Mendl. "I'm sure I saw you yesterday wearing a large cross, begging outside of the church."
"So?" says the beggar. "You think a poor Jew can make a living from just one religion?"

Closely related to the beggar was the shnorrer, the Jew who always found a way to help people part with their money. One such comes regularly to the Rothschild mansion, asking for a handout. Rothschild gives him a donation each week, but, after a while, he tires of it.
The next week, when Rothschild pays the Jew, he says, "Can I give you some advice? I'm not the only wealthy Jew around. Why don't you also ask the others for a contribution?"
The Jew pulls himself up to his full height, such as it is, and replies haughtily, "Mr. Rothschild, I don't tell you how to conduct your business. Please don't tell me how to conduct mine."

A shnorrer, approaching one of his customary handout houses, meets another shnorrer coming out of the house.
"You'd better not ask him for money this week. He's in a foul humor. He only gave me ten rubles."
"So?" replies the latecomer. "Why should I make him a present of ten rubles? Does he give me presents?"

One enterprising shnorrer comes to a Paris antique store with a ratty, old military jacket. "This was worn by Napoleon himself at the Battle of Waterloo. How much will you pay me for such a unique relic?"
"Very interesting," says the proprietor. "But we already have several of Napoleon's jackets. Sorry."

The shnorrer leaves, only to return a week later with an old jar. "This is the very inkwell Victor Hugo used when he wrote *Les Miserables*. I'm willing to let this national treasure go for a reasonable price."

"Thanks very much," says the proprietor. "But we have at least half a dozen of Monsieur Hugo's inkwells."

The shnorrer, much chagrined, stalks out. A week later, he returns with his head swathed in bandages and a small package under his arm.

"Here," says he. "I have the very ear Van Gogh cut off. And don't tell me you already have one because I've got the other one too!"

DEATH

Jews laugh even at death. Why not? Would it change anything if we took it seriously?

Papa, after a long life, is on his deathbed. All the relatives are gathered around. He calls his daughter to his bedside.
"Ruthie, what's that wonderful smell coming from the kitchen?"
"Oh, Mama's baking apple strudel."
"Ruthie, go into the kitchen and get me a piece."
Ruthie goes, but she returns empty-handed.
"Ruthie, where's the strudel?"
"Papa, I'm sorry, but Mama says that's for after."

Herr Salomon is lying on his deathbed in the Jewish Quarter of Old Copenhagen.
"Get the priest. Get the priest," he whispers.
"Don't you mean the rabbi, Papa?"
"No, the priest. Why should I risk giving the rabbi smallpox?"

Yankl, the head of the Burial Society, sees his old friend Yitskhak in the funeral home.
"What are you doing here, Yitskhak?"
"My wife died," replies his friend.
"What are you talking about, Yitskhak? Your dear wife died two years ago."
"That was my first wife. This is my second wife."
"Your second wife?" cries Yankl. "I didn't know you'd remarried. Mazel tov!"[1]

A really nasty fellow dies. The rabbi giving the eulogy has simply nothing good he can honestly say. He turns to the few assembled mourners and asks, "Is there someone here who would like to say a few kind words about the deceased?"
Silence.

---

1. Congratulations

The rabbi implores, "Isn't there anyone who can say something nice about the departed?"
Finally, an old fellow gets up, shuffles forward, steps up to the lectern, looks over the audience, and proclaims, "His bruddeh vas voys."

In the middle of the rabbi's eulogy, a voice shouts from the back of the funeral chapel, "Give him chicken soup!"
"Madam," says the rabbi, "he's dead. It wouldn't help."
"Wouldn't hurt!"

And after death comes the afterlife. Although more focused on the here and now than on the hereafter, Jews still wonder about what comes next. Some of the answers are surprising.

A Hassid dies and awakens to find himself on a beautiful lawn. At the end of the lawn is a kidney-shaped swimming pool. Swimming in the pool is the most beautiful blonde he has ever seen. And sitting on the side of the pool is his lately deceased rebbe, reading the Talmud. As the Hassid looks on in amazement, the blonde gets out of the pool, slithers over to the rebbe in her scanty bikini, and begins blowing in his ear and kissing his body. He continues reading. The Hassid, shocked, approaches the pool and asks, "Rebbe, this is your heaven?"
"No," replies the rebbe, "her hell."

Two Jewish radicals have lived together as a couple for forty years. They both happen to die on the same day, so they meet at the pearly gates. The Angel Gabriel is about to welcome them in when they stop him.
"You know ..." they say. "We were young radicals, and we never got around to getting married. Now we see things differently, and we'd like to enter heaven as husband and wife. Could you please find us a rabbi to perform the ceremony?"
Gabriel disappears. Three days later, he returns with a rabbi, who marries them. Again, Gabriel welcomes them in, but they stop him.
"You know, we were very critical of the government when we were young, but we now see the importance of laws. Could you please find a lawyer who could draw up a document for a civil marriage?"
Gabriel explodes, "It took me three days to find a rabbi up here! You have any idea how long it'll take to find a lawyer?"

Sid and Myra, a pious couple, have debated and argued throughout their marriage about the nature of the afterlife. They finally agree that whoever dies first will try contacting the other with the information. Sid passes on. A few months later, Myra enlists the services of a medium to conjure up Sid's spirit. The séance is arranged. The room is darkened, and the medium calls out, "Sidney, your beloved Myra asks you to communicate with her from the afterlife."

The candles flicker, and Sid's voice is suddenly heard, "Hello, Myra."

"Oh, Sid, tell me about the afterlife," begs Myra.

"Ah, Myra, it's wonderful. I wake up to sunshine every morning. I have breakfast, then I make love, then I have a snack, and then make love again. Lunch and then more lovemaking. Afternoon snack, lovemaking, dinner, one last bout of love, and off to sleep to await the next day."

"That's it?" shouts a highly aggrieved Myra. "That's Oylem Habeh? That's Heaven?"

"I wouldn't know," says Sid's voice. "I've been reincarnated as a jackrabbit in Wyoming."

Sadie Schwab, immigrant from Warsaw to New York City, lives a long, fruitful life and dies in the fullness of years. On the first anniversary of her death, her beloved granddaughter Michelle goes to a famous medium and asks if she can call up the spirit of her late grandmother.

"Of course," says the medium and proceeds to arrange a séance. The assembled all sit, holding hands in the darkened parlor, and the medium intones, "Sadie Schwab, do you have anything to say to your beloved granddaughter?"

The lights flicker, and an ethereal voice says, "Darling Michelle, I miss you very much, but my spirit is at rest. I am happy in the afterlife. Be well, my darling."

The lights flicker on.

"A wonderful encounter," says the medium.

"Yes," muses Michelle, "but when did my grandmother learn to speak English?"

Yudl, a legendary cheapskate, dies, leaving his wife, Bessie, funeral instructions.[2] Afterwards at the shiva, Bessie is talking with her friend Frieda.

"So what did Yudl tell you to do?" asks Frieda.

"Well, he left me three envelopes," explains Bessie. "In the first, I found $20,000 and a note saying, 'Spare no expense on the service.'"

---

2. Seven-day mourning period

"It was indeed a lavish service with a very good eulogy and beautiful flowers," says Frieda.

"In the second envelope," continues Bessie, "I found $35,000 and a note, 'Spare no expense on the cortege.'"

"And indeed you didn't," admits Frieda. "Such a lovely horse-drawn hearse and all those limousines. So what was in the third envelope?"

"Fifty thousand dollars," says Bessie, "and a note, 'Spare no expense on the stone.'"

She holds up her hand, which sports a huge diamond, and asks, "You think it's too ostentatious?"

INTERNECINE HUMOR

"Yidn zaynen a kleyn folk, ober a paskudnye" (Jews are a small people, but an ornery one). No truer epigram was ever spoken. Jews are few in number, often beset by enemies from outside, so what do we do? Pick on each other. Ashkenazim from Europe versus Sephardim from North Africa and the Middle East. Litvaks from Lithuania versus Galitsianers from southeastern Poland. Yeckes from Germany against Ostjuden from Eastern Europe. Religious versus secular Jews, even religious Jews from different denominations. (What's the difference between a *khnyuk*[1] and an *apikoyres*?[2] A *khnyuk* is a Jew who fulfills one more commandment than you. An *apikoyres* is a Jew who fulfills one less.) The only good thing that can be said about this squabbling is that it has proved to be a rich source of humor.

German Jews, Yeckes, are reputedly rigid, humorless, snobbish, and more German than Jewish. Both in Europe and Palestine, to which many of them immigrated in the 1930s (and "brought order" to quote one of my Yecke friends), they suffered the slings and arrows of humorous slander from their fellow Jews.

Why do you never tell a Yecke a joke on Wednesday?
Because his laughter will interrupt the Sabbath service.

What's the difference between a Yecke and a virgin?
Once a Yecke, always a Yecke.

Rumor has it, in 1947, when partition of Palestine into a Jewish and Arab state was considered, the Yeckified town of Nahariya was to wind up in the Arab sector. The townspeople went on strike, under the banner "Nahariya bleibt Deutsch."[3]

---

1. Religious fanatic
2. Heretic
3. German for "Nahariya will remain German." A parody of German nationalism in regions of Europe with German minorities.

The Haifa-Nahariya highway was constructed by Yeckes, passing building stones from hand to hand. It is said, as one approached the project, one heard a constant murmur from the workers. As one got closer, the murmur resolved itself into words.

"Bitte,[4] Herr Doktor."
"Danke,[5] Herr Professor."

For revenge, here's a joke Yeckes told about East European Jews, whom they considered vulgar and dirty:

> Two Ostjuden meet at the bathhouse. One says to the other, "Isn't it amazing how quickly a year goes by?"

A true story:

> My wife's paternal grandmother, a full-blooded Yecke, actually referred to East European Jews (in German) as "nicht unsere," not one of us.

Here's an old riddle:

> Why does God speak Hebrew to the Jews?
> Because if he spoke Yiddish, people would realize he's a Galitsianer.

Jews from other regions looked down upon Galitsianers. Their dialect was considered coarse, and they were thought to be uneducated and vulgar. So, wherein lies the humor? In the first place, the humanization of God. He talks to the Jews. But he chooses Hebrew because his Yiddish is low class. So the first source of amusement is the notion God speaks in a human language. The second is he is a Galitsianer. Who finds this funny? Well, the non-Galitsianers can laugh because even God tries avoiding being taken for a Galitsianer. But the Galitsianers can have the last laugh. God is one of their own.

Galitsianers considered Litvaks to be assimilated to the point of secretly worshiping Jesus. They referred to a Litvak as a tseylem-kop, literally "cross-head."

A Galitsianer boy asks his father, "Why is a Litvak called a tseylem-kop?"

---

4. Please (German)
5. Thank you (German)

"Because," his father replies, "if you take a Litvak and split open his head with an ax, you will find a cross inside."

"But suppose," says the boy, "you split open a Litvak's head and don't find a cross."

"So you're free of one more Litvak."

"Hey, Litvak," shouts a Galitsianer, "you're a tseylem-kop!"

The Litvak replies, "So don't kiss my head."

The first Jewish immigrants to America in the mid-1600s were Sephardim from Holland, where they had come after being driven out of Spain and Portugal by the Inquisition. After them came Ashkenazim, German Jews, in the mid-1800s. From 1881 on, the mass immigration of East European Jews followed. Thus, in America, the Sephardim considered themselves higher-class than the Ashkenazim.

A true story:

> My soon-to-be wife, of part Sephardic origin, met my mother, a born-and-bred New Yorker, and told her, "Our family once lived in New York."
> My mother asked when.
> To which, my fiancée replied, "Well, it wasn't yet called New York."

In France, on the other hand, the old-line Jews are Ashkenazim, while the Sephardim came quite recently as refugees from Arab lands after the creation of the State of Israel.

> A Sephardic Jew in Paris makes a fortune and moves into an elegant building on the posh Avenue Foch. Each day on the stairs, he passes another tenant, an Ashkenazic Jew. The Sephardi always greets the Ashkenazi politely, "Bonjour, Monsieur."
> The Ashkenazi ignores him.
> After some months, the Sephardi has had enough. He confronts the Ashkenazi, "Look here, Monsieur, I greet you politely every day. Why do you refuse to acknowledge me? After all, we are fellow Jews."
> "Monsieur," replies the Ashkenazi, "We have nothing in common culturally. Do you know Beethoven?"
> "No," says the Sephardi.
> "Mozart?"
> "No," says the Sephardi.
> "Schubert?"

"No," says the Sephardi. "But let me ask you. Do you know Ben-Soussan?"[6]
"No," says the Ashkenazi.
"That's too bad," replies the Sephardi. "Because, while you're at the concerts, he's sleeping with your wife."

My father's parents were Polish Jews. My mother's were Romanian Jews. I was therefore quite taken by the French newspaper *Figaro*'s 1999 issue on Jewry, in which this riddle, told by Jews, appeared:

What's the difference between a Polish and a Romanian Jew?
Both will sell their mother and father, but the Polish Jew will deliver the goods.

Most Orthodox Jews view Zionism and the establishment of Israel as manifestations of God's will. They even created religious Zionist political movements, such as Mizrachi. Some Haredim, ultra-Orthodox Jews, on the other hand, reject the idea of a secular Jewish state and await the Messiah, who will then reestablish the Jewish Commonwealth. Many of these very Haredim live in Israel in such cloistered (you should pardon the expression) neighborhoods as Jerusalem's Mea Shearim.

So, the story is told of the Pope's visit to Israel, in which he asks to be taken through Mea Shearim:

> As his entourage passes beneath the window of a Haredi couple, Masha calls to her husband, "Shimke, come look at this! A man with a yarmulke on his head and a cross around his neck!"
> Shimke looks up from his newspaper, and grumbles, "So what can you expect from Mizrachi?"

A variant of this has the ring of truth:

> When Pope John Paul visited Israel, Shimon Peres of the secular Israel Labor Party greeted him. So how could you tell which was the Pope? The one with the yarmulke.

A Jew is shipwrecked on a desert island. He lives there for five years. Finally, a ship comes into view, and a landing party is sent out to rescue him. When

---

6. A typically Sephardic name

they arrive, he shows them around his little island, including the hut he's built, the storage house for vegetables and fruits, and two adjacent mud buildings with crude Jewish stars inscribed over their doorways.
"What's this one?" the captain points to the nearer structure.
"Oh, that's the synagogue where I pray every day."
"And the other one?"
"That's the one I wouldn't set foot into!"

For one-on-one nasty backbiting, nothing can beat Yiddish writers. (Cynthia Ozick captures this in her story "Envy, or Yiddish in America.")

> Two Yiddish writers meet on East Broadway. "Guess what? My readership has doubled in the last year," boasts one.
> Replies the other, "Mazel tov! I didn't know you got married."

Sigmund Freud captured the element of internal contempt in a story he told of a Jew on a train:

> The Jew is stretched out in the compartment with his collar open and feet on the seat. In comes a man in a business suit. The Jew quickly sits up straight and buttons his shirt. The businessman is consulting an appointment book. He turns to the Jew and asks, "Can you tell me when Yom Kippur starts?" The Jew looks at him, opens his collar, and puts his feet back up on the seat. (Get it?)

LOGIC I: TALMUDIC[1] REASONING

Another character providing a great source of humor is the Talmudic reasoner. No topic is too large or too small for these scholars. The humor itself dates back to the Talmud. The Mishnah[2] recounts the following discussion:

> If one finds a small pigeon less than twenty-five meters from a pigeon keeper, it belongs to the pigeon keeper. On the other hand, if one finds it outside the twenty-five-meter limit, it belongs to whoever found it.
>
> "But," asks one rabbi, "if one of the feet is within the twenty-five meters and the other outside, what does one do?"
>
> For posing such a question, the rabbi was thrown out of the house of study.

> A woman confronts her neighbor, "The pot I lent you last week now has a crack in it!"
>
> "I'm innocent," replies the neighbor. "And I can give you three proofs. In the first place, I returned it to you in perfect condition. In the second place, when you lent it to me, it already had a crack. And in the third place, you never lent me a pot in the first place."

> A middle-aged Jew is sitting in a train carriage when a young Jew sits down across from him and asks the time. The elder man ignores him. The young man persists. Finally, the older man replies, "Look, if I tell you the time, you'll thank me. Then I'll feel obliged out of politeness to ask you where you're going. You'll reply you're headed for the same town in which I live. I'll ask what you do, and you'll tell me your goals in life. You'll ask about me and my family, and I'll tell you I have a wife and three daughters, of whom the youngest is not married. You'll ask me about her, and I'll have to tell you

---

1. Referring to the Talmud. Talmudic reasoning implies finely honed logic, also sometimes hairsplitting, which Jews call pilpulistic and non-Jews call Jesuitical.
2. The part of the Talmud that is a direct commentary on the Bible. The other part of the Talmud, the Gemara, is a commentary on and elaboration of the Mishnah.

how beautiful and intelligent she is. You'll express interest, and I'll feel obliged to invite you home to dinner. You and she will fall in love and want to get married. And the last thing I need is for my daughter to be married to someone who can't even afford a watch."

Two business competitors meet on the train.
"Where are you going?" asks Leybl.
"Pinsk," replies Mendl.
Leybl flies into a rage. "You tell me you're going to Pinsk, just so I'll think you're going to Minsk. But I happen to know, in fact, you are going to Pinsk. So why do you lie to me?"

At the beginning of the twentieth century, one Jew asks another, "How does the telegraph work?"
"Imagine," replies his friend, "a dog with its head in Vilna and its tail in Warsaw. If you pull on the tail in Warsaw, the head in Vilna barks."
"Fine," says the first Jew, "but then how does the wireless telegraph work?"
"The same way," comes the reply, "but without the dog."

An interesting new variant:

An Egyptian archaeologist claims the ancient Egyptians had telephones. The proof? He has found the remnant of copper wires in ancient Egyptian tombs. An Israeli archaeologist immediately goes him one better. She has searched ancient Jewish gravesites and found nothing … which proves the Jews had cordless phones.

LOGIC II: GOYISHER KOP, YIDDISHER KOP

The term *Goyisher kop* literally denotes "Gentile head." *Yiddisher kop* means, of course, "Jewish head." The connotations of the former are not complimentary. The simplest usage of *Goyisher kop* is as a synonym for "stupid." Another connotation suggests rigidity in thought patterns. *Yiddisher kop* correspondingly connotes "smart and/or able to think flexibly."

From where did the Jews derive these stereotypes? (Let me be clear at this point. "Tout comprendre n'est pas tout pardonner."[1]) In Eastern Europe, Jews, with universal male literacy and extensive female literacy, found themselves in close contact with usually illiterate, often hostile, Christian peasants. Powerless in the face of the overwhelming numbers of Gentiles, Jews took refuge in touting (to each other) their own educational superiority, which easily degenerated into a notion of inborn intellectual superiority. Hence, the most vulgar connotation of Goyisher kop as simply stupid.

The second connotation, rigidity of thought, is more subtle. Gentiles played by the rules. They respected authority. Jews knew the rules were stacked against them, designed to keep them impoverished and powerless. Eking out a living when most trades, not to mention professions, were closed to you took ingenuity, flexibility of thought, and a nose (pardon the expression) for finding the way over, under, around, or through the wall of persecution. The Yiddish aphorism describing this is "Az me ken nisht ariber, muz men arunter" (If you can't go over, you've got to go under). The closest English proverb is "Where there's a will, there's a way." The cultural context and connotation are not the same.

This survival skill still exists in countries where Jews are persecuted. In societies where they are free, we may nevertheless argue the thought patterns manifest themselves in a unique point of view, one still shaped by marginality and alienation. Philip Roth is not Ernest Hemingway.

---

1. To understand all is not to excuse all. (This is not Yiddish.)

Like Jewish literature and Jewish language, Jewish humor reflects this state of affairs. An example (the only one I know) of the vulgar connotation of *Goyisher kop* is the following:

> A Jew converts to Christianity. The next morning, he wakes up, puts on his tefillin,[2] and begins to daven.
> His wife reminds him, "But you converted yesterday."
> He slaps his forehead and exclaims, "Goyisher kop!"

In my opinion, such jokes about the alleged stupidity of Gentiles do not reflect well on Jews. However, the stupidity of anti-Semites is a popular, legitimate target. We will deal with that in the Anti-Semites section.

The more interesting jokes of this Goyisher Kop, Yiddisher Kop genre are those in which the Jews laugh at their own bigotry.

> Two Jews are driving through the Polish countryside in their horse-drawn wagon when they come upon a fallen log blocking the road. They descend, look over the log, and begin discussing strategy.
> "According to Rabbi Yekhezkl of Plotsk," says the one, "a fallen log must have its branches removed before one attempts to move it."
> "But," replies the other, "Rabbi Yehoshua of Kotsk says, on the contrary, the trunk should be lifted first before any branches are removed."
> So they argue for a full hour. A Polish peasant comes by in his wagon. He descends, releases his horse's reins from the wagon, attaches them to the log, and shouts "Giddap!" The horse drags the log to the side of the road. The peasant reattaches the horse to his wagon and drives on. The Jews look after him.
> "Big deal," says one. "Brute force."

This is characteristic of many stories in which Jews laugh at themselves for misapplying the Yiddisher kop while simultaneously mocking the useful skills of the Gentiles as Goyisher kop. (Mendele Moykher Sforim, the "Grandfather of Yiddish Literature," parodies this in his novel, *The Travels of Benjamin the Third*.) Here's another:

> It's 1920. Berl and Shmerl are discussing who is the smartest of the smart.
> "The Jews, of course," says Berl.

---

2. Phylacteries; boxes with Scriptural writings observant Jews put on their head and left arm while reciting the morning prayers

"But which Jews?" asks Shmerl.
"The Zionists," says Berl.
"But which Zionists?" persists Shmerl.
"The Russian Zionists."
"But which Russian Zionists?"
"The Russian Labor Zionists."
"But which of them?"
"The Odessa Russian Labor Zionists."
"And of them?"
"Their leader, Mendl Shumacher," says Berl.
"Oh yeh, I know him," says Shmerl. "What an idiot!"

In the category in which *Yiddisher kop* means "seeing things in a different, more flexible way," for better or worse, we have the following:

A priest, a minister, and a rabbi are playing their customary Wednesday game of golf. In front of them is an incredibly slow foursome. So much so, the three clergymen finally complain to the manager, who tells them, "This is a new program we have. Those are blind golfers. There is a guide with them and some devices that allow them to track the sound of the ball. But they do play slowly. I hope you can understand and be patient."
The minister, chagrined, exclaims, "I can't believe my own insensitivity. Sunday, I shall give a sermon on charity and tolerance."
The priest, equally upset, says, "And I shall ask my parishioners to join me in donating time and money to the blind."
The rabbi turns to the manager and asks, "Why can't they play at night?"

A variant of this, without the cultural context, has come over the Web:

Stevie Wonder challenges Jack Nicklaus to a game of golf. Stevie sets the stakes at $10,000. The astonished Nicklaus asks Stevie how he can play, and Stevie explains a guide is with him, as well as some devices that allow him to track the sound of the ball.
"Okay," says Nicklaus, "When do you want to play?"
"Any night next week," answers Stevie.

A couple is in bed in the middle of the night. She nudges him awake and tells him, "Get up and close the window. It's cold outside."

Angry at being peremptorily awakened, he jumps out of bed, stomps over to the window, slams it shut, and says to her, "Okay, so I closed the window. Now it's warm outside?"

Mrs. Levine is preparing for her daughter's bat mitzvah.[3] She calls Mrs. Weinstein. "You had your daughter's bat mitzvah at the same place we are, and you had the same caterer. And you had 200 guests, the same as we're having. Let me ask you, how much fish did you order? How much bread? And how much wine?"

"Oh," says Mrs. Weinstein, "we ordered forty pounds of fish, seventy-five loaves of bread, and fifty bottles of wine."

Mrs. Levine follows suit. After the gala event, she realizes half of everything is left over. She calls Mrs. Weinstein. "I bought the amounts you told me, and we had twice as much as we needed."

"Yes," replies Mrs. Weinstein, "so did we."

Yente and Yakhne are walking down the street when it begins raining.
"Quick, Yente, open your umbrella," says Yakhne.
"It wouldn't help," replies Yente. "It's full of holes."
"So why did you bring an umbrella with holes?" asks Yakhne.
Yente sighs. "So who knew it was going to rain?"

Feinstein knocks on the door of his neighbor, Goldstein.
"Come in," says Goldstein.
Feinstein enters to see Goldstein sitting in his reading chair, stark naked except for a hat. "Goldstein, why are you sitting there naked?"
"Why not?" says Goldstein, "I'm not expecting visitors."
"But why the hat?" asks Feinstein.
"Just in case someone comes," says Goldstein.

A Jew newly arrived in America takes a package to the post office to send home to his family. He puts what he thinks is the right postage on it, but the clerk weighs it and says, "It's too heavy. You'll have to add a dollar's worth of stamps."

"And how," asks the Jew, "will that make it lighter?"

---

3. Confirmation service for thirteen-year-old females; cf. bar mitzvah for males

Here's a story North African Jews tell about their folk hero, Djoha (and also Polish Jews tell about theirs, Hershele Ostropolier):

> Djoha is very poor. He keeps the little money he has managed to accumulate in a locked box. One night, a noise awakens him and his wife. They rush down the stairs to find a thief has run off with the box. His wife begins crying, but Djoha is smiling.
> "What are you smiling about," she asks through her tears.
> Djoha chuckles, "He may have gotten the box, but I still have the key!"

> In Czarist Russia, four men—a Russian, a Pole, a Ukrainian, and a Jew—are arrested for illegal gambling at cards. They're taken into the court and put in the dock one by one.
> The judge asks the Russian, "Were you playing cards?"
> "No, I swear it," he replies.
> The judge asks the Pole.
> Again, "No."
> And the same with the Ukrainian.
> Finally, it's the Jew's turn.
> "Were you playing cards?" asks the judge.
> The Jew replies, "With who?"

> Napoleon's army wins a great victory, and three soldiers—a Prussian, a Pole, and a Jew—are the heroes of that battle. Napoleon calls them before him and asks each what reward he would like.
> "A free Prussia!" cries the Prussian.
> "Done!" says Napoleon.
> He asks the Pole, who replies, "A restored Kingdom of Poland!"
> "Done!" says the emperor.
> He turns to the Jew.
> "A piece of fried herring on rye bread every Friday," says the Jew.
> "Done!" says Napoleon.
> When the Jew returns to his barracks, his comrades ask him how he could be so thickheaded. "The Prussian asks for Prussian independence. The Pole requests the restoration of Polish sovereignty. And all you can think to ask for is fried herring?"
> The Jew smiles. "Chances are, I'll get the herring."

Three nuclear scientists—an American, a Norwegian, and an Israeli—accidentally get an overdose of radiation. They're rushed to the hospital, where the doctor diagnoses their illness as fatal.
"Any last wishes?" ask their distraught colleagues.
The American answers, "To be buried with honors in Arlington Cemetery."
The Norwegian says, "To lie at rest in my beloved Oslo, by the fjord."
The Israeli replies, "A second opinion."

LOGIC III: THIS YOU CALL LOGIC?

A Jew comes upon his friend lying across the track of the single railway that passes by their shtetl.
"Moishe, what are you doing?" he demands.
"Committing suicide," replies Moishe.
"But what's that sack in your hand?"
"My lunch."
"Your lunch?"
"Yeh, until the train comes through here, a person could die of hunger."

Two fellows are standing in midtown Manhattan when they hear faint strains of music from above. They look up and see a guy walking a tightrope strung across two skyscrapers while playing the violin.
"Wow," says one. "What do you think of that?"
The other sniffs, "Paganini he's not."

A Jewish social club in Paris decides to climb an Alp. They get themselves all outfitted, drive to Chamonix at the foot of Mont Blanc, and begin their ascent. Halfway up, snow begins falling. One hour later, they can see nothing and realize they'd better find shelter quickly. Luckily, they find a fully stocked, fully insulated climbers' cabin nearby, where they bed down for the night.
Meanwhile, down in Chamonix, the people realize the group has not returned. They call the Red Cross, which organizes a rescue team to scale the mountain at dawn. After an arduous climb, the rescuers spy the cabin with smoke rising from its chimney. They make their way over and knock on the door.
"Who is it?" asks a voice from inside.
"Red Cross."
"Oh," says the voice, "we already gave."

At a senior citizens' club in Miami Beach, the widow Birnbaum notices a new fellow sitting off to the side. He is tall and distinguished with a mane of white hair and a nice suit. She walks over and sits down.
"Are you new here?"
"Yes," he replies, "I just moved down to Florida."
"May I ask from where?" says Mrs. Birnbaum.
"Joliet, Illinois."
"And may I ask, what you did there?" she persists.
"I was in prison."
"Really? For how long, if I may ask?"
"Twenty-five years," he replies."
"Twenty-five years? May I ask, if you won't take offense, for what crime?"
"I murdered and dismembered my wife," he replies.
"Ah," says Mrs. Birnbaum, "so you're single?"

Mr. and Mrs. Cohen are getting ready to go out for dinner in Miami.
"Should I wear the diamond bracelet or the 14-karat gold?" she asks.
"Either. Just get dressed!"
"Should I wear the cultured pearl necklace?"
"Doesn't matter. Get ready."
"You think it's cold enough for the mink coat, or is the sable stole enough?"
"Listen," he retorts, "If we don't go right now, we're gonna miss the early bird special!"

HERETICS, ATHEISTS, FREETHINKERS, CONVERTS

As the European Enlightenment worked its way east, it captured the minds and the hearts of many Jews. Today, all except the ultra-Orthodox are products of that Enlightenment. Modern Jewish life represents a constant creative tension between the traditional and the modern world, one in which Jews are no longer isolated from Gentiles. This process, begun several hundred years ago, rapidly accelerated in the nineteenth and twentieth centuries. Sholem Aleikhem's *Tevye the Dairyman*, popularized in *Fiddler on the Roof*, is a novel about the struggle between the old world and the new.

This struggle gave rise to a great deal of humor, as young Jews rebelled against their traditions. Heretics, atheists, so-called freethinkers, and even converts to Christianity came in for their share. (We must note the first three have been integrated into Jewish life. The converts have been rejected. Even when they masquerade as "Jews for Jesus" or "Messianic Jews.") Two themes dominate. The first is chutzpah.[1] If you're going to be a rebel, then no half-measures. In for a penny, in for a pound. Or, as the Yiddish expression has it, "Az men est khazer, zol es rinen iber der bord un di peyes" (If you're going to eat pork, then let it run down your beard and earlocks). However, within this aphorism also lies the second theme. Even the rebellious Jew can't quite escape his (or her?) "beard and earlocks."

The first thing at risk was Halakhah,[2] usually the eating of kosher food. That's why, if you want to find a good Chinese restaurant, go to a Jewish neighborhood. Those wontons look like kreplekh,[3] but that isn't a cow's oink you're hearing.

---

1. Gall, only more so. Gall ain't nothing compared to *chutzpah*.
2. Jewish law
3. Dumplings

In fact, because Chinese civilization dates back to the Shang Dynasty (about 1600 BCE[4]) while Jewish civilization dates back to Abraham (1850 BCE), one wonders, "What did we eat for the first 250 years?"

A Jew travels every week on business from his shtetl to a nearby town. On the road is a Gentile restaurant. The most enticing aroma, roast pig, comes from that restaurant. The Jew resists the Yeytser Hore (the evil inclination) as long as he can, but he succumbs to temptation one day, enters the restaurant, and orders the roast pig. After a brief wait, out it comes—a crisp, little piglet surrounded by all the trimmings with an apple in its mouth. He takes one bite and is lost forever.

Each week, he returns for the same order. Each week, it comes out, done to perfection, complete with trimmings and the apple in its mouth. One day, the Jew has just placed his order when he spies at a nearby table, a fellow Jew, from his own shtetl, drinking a glass of tea. What to do? Out comes the roast piglet with the trimmings and apple in its mouth. Our hero looks at the dish, turns to his acquaintance, and remarks, "Order a baked apple around here, and look at the fuss they make!"

A Hassid in full battle dress—shtrayml,[5] kapote,[6] beard, and peyes[7]—enters a supermarket, goes up to the appetizing counter, points at the baked Virginia ham, and says to the clerk, "I'd like a pound of that nice kosher turkey."

"But, sir," replies the clerk, "that's not turkey. It's ham."

The Hassid fixes her with a cold stare. "Did I ask you?"

A Christian friend invites a religious Jew home. The Christian serves a beautiful roast chicken, but the Jew demurs.

"I cannot eat nonkosher food."

"Are there no conditions under which you can violate that ban?" asks the Christian as he continues partaking of the chicken.

"Oh, yes," says the Jew. "When one's life is at stake, one must eat whatever is at hand."

---

4. Before the Common Era. Jews don't use BC because Christ means Messiah, and we are still waiting for the First Coming of ours. Similarly, we use CE, Common Era, rather than AD, "Year of our Lord." Actually, with the new wave of multicultural sensitivity, BCE and CE are becoming standard usage.
5. Fur hat
6. Long gabardine; caftan
7. Earlocks; singular is *peye*.

> With that, the Christian whips out a pistol, points it at the Jew, and says, "Eat some of this chicken, or I'll kill you!"
> The terrified Jew proceeds to devour a thigh, a leg, and half the breast. The Christian lowers his gun and says, "I was kidding. I would never shoot you. I just wanted to test whether you would obey your laws."
> "You know what?" says the Jew, "The next time you want to play these games, how about starting while the chicken is still hot?"

> The Yom Kippur service is suddenly interrupted by a Jew staggering into the synagogue, crying, "Water, I'm dying, give me water!"
> Although it is forbidden to eat or drink anything on Yom Kippur, the saving of a life takes precedence over such an injunction. The congregation carries the man to a bench, and the rabbi himself gives the unfortunate a glass of water. He drinks it down in one gulp, turns to the rabbi, and says, "Oh, thank you! You have saved my life. And, in return, I promise to never again eat herring on Yom Kippur!"

Just because Jews became enlightened didn't mean they lost their skill at Talmudic reasoning.

> A freethinker is caught eating on Tsom Gedaliah, the Fast of Gedaliah, between Rosh Hashonah and Yom Kippur. He is brought before the rabbi, who asks him to explain why he violated the fast.
> "I have three explanations," replies the freethinker. "First, why do we fast on Tsom Gedaliah? Because we commemorate the death of Gedaliah, the Jewish puppet governor of Judea under Roman occupation, who was assassinated by nationalist zealots. So, if he hadn't been assassinated, would he be alive today? No. So why should I fast? Second, if I had been the one assassinated, would Gedaliah be fasting for me? No. So why should I fast for him? But third and most important, why should I fast on Tsom Gedaliah when I'm going to be eating on Yom Kippur?"

Jewish secularists in the late nineteenth and early twentieth centuries made it a matter of principle to violate the laws of eating kosher, not smoking or riding on the Sabbath and holy days, observing various fast days, and many other injunctions.

> Two Jewish secularists are boasting about their practices.
> "Every Yom Kippur, instead of fasting, I eat a ham sandwich with all the trimmings," proudly proclaims the first.

"Ha, I'm more of an *apikoyres* than you," announces the other. "On Pesakh, every day for lunch, instead of matzoh, I eat a bacon cheeseburger on a white bun."

"That's nothing" is the rejoinder. "Every Tisha B'av,[8] I eat an entire roast goose."

"Feh," says the second. "You know what I eat on Tisha B'av? Just a little kashe[9] with milk. By me, Tisha B'av isn't even a yontev[10] any more."

Those last three stories are from the old country and the nineteenth century. Here are a couple of modern *apikoyres'* tales:

A Jew phones his son and reminds him, "Yom Kippur starts tomorrow."
The son replies, "Bet a hundred on him—win, place, or show."

A Jew is walking to synagogue on Yom Kippur. He passes a seafood restaurant and looks in to see his friend and fellow Jew eating that least kosher of dishes, oysters.
"How can you eat oysters on Yom Kippur?" he exclaims.
"Why not?" replies the friend, "Yom Kippur ends in an 'r.'"

Mrs. Cohen, recently immigrated to the United States, is sitting in a park on New York's Lower East Side one Shabbes when she notices a well-dressed, middle-aged man reading the Yiddish newspaper *Der Forverts*[11] on an adjacent bench. He takes out a cigar and lights it up. Mrs. Cohen, observant in both senses of the word, looks on. Finally, she shakes her head in awe. "America, truly an amazing land. Even the goyim[12] read Yiddish!"

---

8. The ninth day of the Jewish month Av. (It usually occurs in midsummer.) A major fast day of the Jewish year, it commemorates the destruction of both Jewish temples (587 BCE and 70 CE) and a series of other catastrophes.
9. Buckwheat groats, a simple dish
10. Festive day; holiday
11. *The Forward*. This secular Jewish newspaper, once a daily, is now published weekly. Today, it is referred to as *Der Forverts*, without translation, because an English-language Jewish newspaper is called *The Forward*.
12. Gentiles; plural of *goy*

While we're mentioning *Der Forverts*, Jews ask a droll question: How is it that the *New York Times* knows what *Der Forverts* will be printing three days in advance?

> Goldstein goes to the judge. In his rich Yinglish[13] accent, he says, "I vant to change my name to Murphy."
> The judge gives him his new name. One year later, he's back.
> "I vant to change my name again. To Johnson."
> "Why?" asks the judge. "You just changed it a year ago."
> "Yeh, but, every time I introduced myself as Murphy, people asked, 'Vat vas it before?' I had to tell them Goldstein. Now, I'll introduce myself as Johnson. Ven dey ask vat it vas before, I can say Murphy."

The convert to Christianity is not highly regarded by his or her former fellow Jews. The act is usually interpreted to smack more of treason, denial of one's origins, and social climbing than of conviction. Coupled to this is the belief that even the converted Jew is still a Jew in the eyes of the Gentiles. From these strong and complex feelings comes a humor that mocks attempts at assimilation through conversion. Despite the best efforts of the convert, the enterprise is sooner or later doomed to failure.

> Two Jews decide to convert to Christianity in the old country. Off they go to the Russian priest and get the deed done.
> As they leave the church, one says to the other, "I don't think it took. I still can't stand the thought of eating pork."
> "I know," says the other. "I'm still afraid of dogs."

> A Polish Jew converts to Catholicism in the nineteenth century. The first Friday after the conversion, the priest stops by the home of his new congregant to see how he's doing. The congregant is sitting at the table, happily eating a slab of boiled beef.
> "What are you doing?" exclaims the priest. "Don't you remember I told you we don't eat meat on Friday?"
> "It's not meat," says the convert. "It's fish."
> The priest says, "What are you talking about? I can see it's meat. How can you say it's fish?"
> "Simple," replies the convert. "I just did what you did. You took me to the baptismal font, sprinkled holy water over my head, and said, 'You're a Chris-

---

13. Mixture of Yiddish and English

tian.' I took the piece of beef to the same font, sprinkled holy water on it, and proclaimed, 'You're a fish.'"

Then there's the ambivalent attitude of the French Jewish community toward the late Cardinal Jean-Marie Lustiger, the converted son of Polish Jews. All agree he was a fine man and a great defender of the Jews, but still.... They have the following riddle:

Why is the Chief Rabbi of France a Sephardi?
Because the Cardinal of Paris was an Ashkenazi.

A Jewish hunchback and a Jewish convert are walking down the street. They pass the local synagogue.
"You know," says the convert, "I used to be a Jew."
"You know," says the hunchback, "I used to be a hunchback."

A Jewish convert takes on the profession of preacher. He goes around to the various East European Jewish communities, preaching the Gospel, and trying to get the Jews to convert. At one such encounter, he meets his match. Every claim he makes is disputed by audience members, who show it to be illogical or false. After an hour of this, he finally exclaims, "What's the matter with you people? Can't you let a poor Jew make a living?"

The convert is also the subject (some might say the butt) of American Jewish humor.

A Jew goes to a minister and asks to be converted.
"Before I do so," says the minister. "I need to know if you are familiar with the basic facts of our faith. Where was Jesus born?"
The Jew thinks for a minute and answers, "Pittsburgh."
"You can't be serious!" exclaims the minister.
"Maybe it was Philadelphia," hazards the potential convert.
The minister shakes his head. "Sorry, but you have so little knowledge that I simply cannot support your conversion."
"Okay," says the Jew, "So where was Jesus born?"
"Bethlehem," replies the minister.
"Well at least I knew it was Pennsylvania."

Here's an acerbic little twist on anti-Semitism:

> Three Jews pass a church with a sign outside saying, "We will pay you $1,000 if you convert." One of the Jews volunteers to go in and see if the offer is serious. He comes out a half hour later.
> "Did they convert you?" ask his comrades.
> "Indeed they did," he replies.
> "And did they pay you the $1,000?"
> The new convert looks at his former coreligionists. "Is that all you people ever think about?"

A small Brooklyn yeshivah[14] suddenly receives a check for $100,000 from one Benjamin Sheinblatt with a note thanking them for educating his son. The head of the yeshivah calls Mr. Sheinblatt to thank him, but he admits he doesn't recall his son.

"Ah," says Benjamin Sheinblatt. "Nevertheless, you have done me and the Jewish people a great favor. My son fell in love with a young woman whose father is a noted Presbyterian minister. When my boy met the family, the father told him, 'Although I would have preferred my daughter marry a Christian, I am willing to accept you if I am convinced you are well-educated in your own faith. Who was the founder of the Jewish religion?' My son didn't know. 'Then who,' asked the minister, 'led the Hebrews out of Egypt?' Again my son didn't know. Finally, the minister asked, 'What is the Talmud?' Again, my son didn't know. So the minister refused the match.

If it weren't for the education you gave my son, he'd be married to a shikse."

---

14. Institution of higher Jewish learning

SMALL BUSINESS, BIG BUSINESS—WAITERS, SEAMSTRESSES, TAILORS, CABBIES, AND OTHER ENTREPRENEURS

In each country where Jews have lived, they have been found in certain trades and businesses. Usually it was not by choice. In Christian and Muslim countries, Jews were restricted to certain jobs the majority chose not to do. In America as well, many professions were closed to Jews until relatively recently. These restrictions and the widespread poverty they caused led to the need for finding the few available niches. Once we had done this, what happened? The anti-Semites wanted to know, "How come you people are so good at business? Are you born with a special attachment to money?" It's easy to find anti-Semitic jokes about Jews and business. But, feh, who needs them?

However, there are also Jewish jokes about these topics. They have an entirely different tone. Some are stories of typical Jewish occupations, like waiter, tailor, peddler, or seamstress. Others deal with the thin line between success and poverty for the Jewish entrepreneur. Still others celebrate cleverness, but without the nasty bite of the anti-Semite. Some even do a reverse twist on the stereotype. Here's one:

> Eight-year-old Wilbur Smedley III comes to his friend Sammy Kaplan and says, "My parents say I can't play with you anymore because you're Jewish." Sammy replies, "Tell them we're not playing for money."

Jewish waiters are the stuff of which legend is made. Competence? Of the highest order. Finesse? Even politeness? That's a different story:

> Max the waiter comes over to the table of a really sad-looking customer. "What'll you have?"

> "A bowl of kreplekh soup and a few kind words," is the reply. Max goes off to the kitchen and comes back with the soup. He plunks it down on the table and walks away.
> "What about the few kind words?" asks the customer.
> Max calls over his shoulder, "Don't eat the soup."

> Two guys go into the Delancey Street Delicatessen.
> "What'll youse have?" snaps Max the waiter.
> "I'll have a glass of tea," says one.
> "Me, too," says the other. "And make sure the glass is clean."
> Max returns a minute later with the tea and asks, "Who ordered the clean glass?"

Tailoring was also a popular Jewish trade, especially among immigrants to America. Those who had to learn the skill here were actually called Columbuses shnayders (Columbus's tailors).[1]

> Mr. Faynshmecker brings a bolt of cloth to Levine the tailor and asks him to make a suit. Levine does all the measurements.
> "When can it be ready?" asks Faynshmecker.
> "In three weeks," answers Levine.
> "Three weeks? But the Lord made the entire world in six days."
> "Yeh," says Levine, "but look at my suits, and look at the world."

> Mr. Faynshmecker brings a bolt of cloth to Levine the tailor and asks him to make a suit. Levine does all the measurements.
> "Sorry," says Levine, "not enough material."
> So, Faynshmecker takes the bolt of cloth across the road to Korngold, the other tailor, and asks him to make a suit. Korngold takes the measurements and makes the suit.
> Faynshmecker wears his new suit to a dinner at the Jewish Community Center, where he not only encounters Levine, but Korngold and Korngold's six-year-old son, who is wearing a suit identical to Faynshmecker's.
> Faynshmecker collars Levine and asks, "What kind of a tailor are you? You told me you didn't have enough material to make this suit. Korngold not only had enough for my suit, but he had enough left over for his little boy."
> "Sure," replies Levine. "He has a little boy. I have a big boy."

---

1. This has nothing to do with any of the jokes. I just thought you might like to know.

Pauline, a retired seamstress, is walking down Fifth Avenue when a man in a raincoat suddenly opens it wide and exposes himself. She peers closely and remarks, "That you call a lining?"

For forty years, Abe Feldman eked out a living in his dry-cleaning store in London. Suddenly, China takes over Hong Kong. The next thing he knows, immigrants from Hong Kong buy the empty warehouse to the left of his shop and open a large dry cleaning establishment.

One month later, another family of Hong Kong immigrants buys the warehouse on the other side … and open a dry cleaning establishment as well.

Abe's children are worried and call their father.

"How are you doing, Dad? Can you survive?"

"Survive?" says Abe. "Business couldn't be better."

"But Dad, how is that possible?"

"I put up a new sign over my door," says Abe. "Main Entrance."

Two immigrant Jews are learning English. One asks the other, "Can you explain me what means alternative?"

"Sure," replies the other. "Just imagine, you, a poor Jew, are walking down the street here in New York City, and you see a twenty-dollar bill on the ground. You pick it up, go to the market, and buy a rooster and a hen. The hen begins laying eggs, which you sell. Thanks to the rooster, some of the eggs hatch. You have more chickens and then more hens, more eggs, and more roosters. Business prospers. You buy a nice piece of farmland in New Jersey. You build a house and a chicken coop. You keep doing better and better. Then, one day, along comes a downpour. The flood destroys your house and drowns all the chickens. You're a poor Jew again."

"Yeh," asks the first Jew. "So what does this have to do with the meaning of alternative?"

"Ducks."

The Jewish cabdriver is also a character of legend. Equally colorful characters of other ethnicities have now largely replaced him, but his soul goes marching on.

A rabbi dies and finds himself in a long line at the pearly gates. A group of angels suddenly rushes out and escorts in a fellow who was several people behind him.

"Who's he to get such special treatment?" the rabbi asks a nearby angel.

"Oh, he was a cab driver."

"A cabbie? How come he takes precedence over a rabbi?"

"Because," replies the angel, "he put the fear of God into more people in one day than you did in your entire life!"

A young woman hails a cab on Fifth Avenue.
"How do I get to Carnegie Hall?" she asks the cabbie.
"Practice!"

A fellow hails a cab at Rockefeller Center in Manhattan.
"Where to, buddy?"
'The Palmer House," replies the customer.
"Where's that?"
"Chicago."
"Chicago? Why don't you fly or take the train?"
"Don't like either. If you'll take me, I'll pay you double the fare plus a twenty-five percent tip."
"Okay," agrees the cabbie. "Give me directions."
So off they go, down the West Side Highway to the Lincoln Tunnel, over to Route 95 to Route 80 through Pennsylvania, across the Ohio and Indiana Turnpikes, over the Chicago Skyway, up the Dan Ryan Expressway, east to Lake Shore Drive, off at Monroe, and then south on Wabash to the Palmer House. Sixteen hours. The customer gets out, pays the promised double fare and tip, and walks into the hotel. Two ladies run over to the cab and start to get in.
"Where to?" asks the cabbie.
"Flatbush Avenue," they reply. "We'll pay you triple the fare plus thirty percent tip."
"Sorry," says the cabbie. "I don't go to Brooklyn."

The old country version of the cabbie was the *balagole*,[2] the wagon driver:

One such, Yankl, agrees to take Leybl the cloth wholesaler to Minsk. It's winter, the road is long, there's snow everywhere, and Yankl's horse is no spring chicken.
After about three miles, Yankl says to Leybl, "Look, there's a steep hill just ahead. I'm afraid it's too much for my poor beast. Can we get down and walk up the hill?"
Leybl agrees.

---

2. Pronounced bah-la-GOH-leh

After another few miles, Yankl again turns to Leybl. "You can see my poor horse is tired. If she could only walk without the burden of passengers for the next two miles or so, I think she could catch her breath."
Again Leybl agrees.
And so it goes, on and off—more off than on—for the rest of the trip. As the towers of Minsk come into view, Leybl says to Yankl, "Please explain me something. I'm going to Minsk because I have business there. You're going because I hired you to drive me. But for what reason is your horse going to Minsk?"

Entrepreneurial spirit is not a Jewish invention, but it certainly provides some good Jewish jokes.

Cohen immigrates to New York City and starts out as an itinerant ribbon peddler. Through dint of hard work and a bit of luck, he eventually becomes the largest ribbon wholesaler in America. He sells to all the biggest department stores—with the exception of the anti-Semitic Snodgrass & Co. in Chicago. Just before he retires, Cohen makes one final attempt. He flies out to Chicago, literally camps on Snodgrass's doorstep, and demands an order. Snodgrass, as usual, refuses. But Cohen persists.
"Mr. Snodgrass, it's my last wish. Believe me, I'll take any order, no matter how large or how small!"
"Okay, Cohen, it's a deal, just to get rid of you," says Snodgrass. He grabs an order form and writes, "Snodgrass and Co. will purchase as much ribbon as stretches from the tip of Cohen's Jewish nose to the tip of his Jewish penis." Three weeks later, Snodgrass gets a call from the loading dock. Four truckloads of ribbons have just arrived from Cohen's in New York City. Snodgrass, furious, calls Cohen.
"Don't you pull this on me, you lying Jew. I know just what I ordered!"
Cohen replies, "The tip of my nose is right here with me in New York City. The tip of my penis is in Kiev."

Best friends Moishe and Chaim, two Polish Jews, survive the ghettos and the camps and start their lives over after the war. Moishe moves to New York City; Chaim goes to Paris. Twenty years pass, and they lose track of each other. One day, a telegram arrives at Chaim's little delicatessen in the Marais:[3] "Chaim: I have made it very big. I own Best Ice Cream, the largest ice cream company in America. I have missed you and wish you could share

---

3. Jewish neighborhood in Paris

my good fortune. If you are willing, reply yes to this messenger, and I will bring you over to New York City."

Chaim thinks about it briefly and says yes. In short order, his few worldly goods are packed, and he is driven to Charles De Gaulle Airport, where he flies first class to JFK. From there, a stretch limo whisks him into Manhattan and up Madison Avenue to an enormous building. Best Ice Cream, Inc. He is taken up the private elevator to the penthouse. As he approaches the president's office, he reads the sign on the door: "Best Ice Cream, Inc. We don't sell to Jews." Aghast and furious, he knocks. His old friend Moishe opens the door and rushes to greet him ... to be met with a slap in the face.

"You, Moishe? After all we suffered together? You should have such a sign? We Don't Sell to Jews?"

"Hold on," replies Moishe. "Have you tasted this ice cream?"

Marvin and Harold's Women's Fashions, Fifth Floor, 498 Seventh Avenue, in New York's Garment Center, is struggling through another bad year. Their competitors are flourishing while they lose money every day. Finally, Marvin can't take it any more. He rides the elevator to the twenty-third floor, climbs the stairs to the roof, takes one last look around, and jumps. Of course, on his way down, he passes the windows of all the other companies. As he shoots past the fifth floor, he shouts in to Harold, "Cut velvet!"

Marvin's suicide attempt fails. He lands on a pile of returns.

Sam and Hesh, two furriers, meet on Seventh Avenue one January day.
"How's business?" asks Sam.
"What can I say?" answers Hesh. "You know how it is in January. Everyone wants their fur yesterday."
"Yeh, I know," says Sam. "But at least you got your partner Morris to help with the orders."
"Morris died last week," says Hesh.
"What!" replies Sam. "Right in the middle of high season?"

Lou and Hymie, two men's suit retailers, meet on Seventh Avenue one January day. "How's business?" asks Lou.
"You know how it is," replies Hymie. "It's terrible!"
"But the president says business has never been better," protests Lou.
"Yeh?" retorts Hymie. "The president must have a better location."

Rabbi Silverman gets a visit from one of his congregants, Al Goldstein, a prosperous businessman. Except it turns out he isn't.

"Rabbi, my business is failing, my creditors are going to repossess my car, the bank is foreclosing on my house, and my wife is so unhappy about it that she's threatened to leave me. What can I do?"

"Well, Al," says the rabbi, "whenever I need a source of solace and wisdom, I take down a volume of the Talmud, close my eyes, open it at random, put my finger down on the page, and read what it says. I trust in the Lord to help me. Why don't you go in to the synagogue library and try it?"

Al is pretty skeptical, but he agrees to give it a shot. That's the last Rabbi Silverman thinks of the matter until three months later when he's walking down the street and hears a car horn. He turns around, and it's Al Goldstein, greeting him from the driver's seat of a new BMW convertible.

"Rabbi, I can't thank you enough! I took your advice. As you can see, it's completely changed my life! Finances in good shape. Marriage couldn't be better!"

The rabbi, intrigued, asks, "So what were the first words you saw in the Talmud?"

"Chapter Eleven."

Chatskl, a poor shtetl Jew, hears tell of a strange land in which the inhabitants have never seen an onion. He gathers up a wagonload and drives off in search of that benighted country. After many days, he arrives and quickly sets up business, showing the king and his subjects how to raise, cook, and eat onions with meat, with fish, in salad, or by themselves. The people are thrilled beyond belief. Rewarded with a wagonload of gold, Chatskl returns to his shtetl a rich man.

Itsik, also a poor Jew, is amazed and more than a little jealous of his friend Chatskl. But the latter reassures him, "Listen, Itsik, they've also never heard of garlic. You can make a killing."

Itsik gathers up a wagonload of garlic and drives off. He arrives and quickly sets up business, showing the king and his subjects how to raise, cook, and eat garlic. The people are thrilled beyond belief. They reward him with a wagonload of onions.

"You wouldn't believe what happened to me," says Grandpa Moishe, late of Czarist Russia, lately of Santa Fe, New Mexico. "Shortly after I arrived here sixty years ago, I was driving through the desert when I was suddenly surrounded by a large party of Indians armed with tomahawks."

"What did you do, Grandpa?"

"What could I do? I bought three bead necklaces and a blanket."

Chaim comes to Yekhiel with a great deal.

"My friend, have I got a bargain for you! For only $5,000, a genuine African elephant!"

"Are you meshuge?" says Yekhiel. "What would I do with an elephant? I live in a one-bedroom apartment."

"This is a beautiful, strong, intelligent elephant," persists Chaim.

"My apartment is on the fourth floor of a walk-up building. You're talking craziness! What do I need with such a thing?"

"Listen," says Chaim, "I also have a baby elephant, cute as a button. You can have both for only $7,000."

"Now," says Yekhiel, "you're beginning to interest me."

The rabbi is called upon to settle a business dispute between Rakhmiel and Mendl, two of his congregants.

"Before we start, Rabbi," says Rakhmiel, "I simply want to ask you some questions. Is white a color?"

The rabbi ponders for a minute. "Yes, white is indeed a color."

"What about black?" persists Rakhmiel. "Is black a color?"

Again the rabbi ponders. "Yes, I must say black is also a color."

"You see?" Rakhmiel turns triumphantly to Mendl. "I sold you a color TV!"

OUR PAL, GOD

Jews have a paradoxical relationship with God. We might call it skeptical reverence. We are less servants than partners and not entirely silent partners, to say the least. From the time Abraham went mano a mano with God about Sodom, Jews have continued to argue and question. (There's an old Yiddish expression, "If God lived on earth, people would break his windows.")

> Every day as he goes to his business in Copenhagen, Herr Salomon passes a lovely restaurant. It's got a wonderful aroma, and he knows what it is, that world-renowned Danish ham. One sunny spring day, the restaurant windows are open, and the aroma proves irresistible. In goes Herr Salomon and orders a skinke smørrebrød, an open-faced ham sandwich. He eats it in three bites, pays, and heads for the door.
> As he reaches the street, the sky turns black, and a peal of thunder shakes the sky.
> Herr Salomon looks up and says, "Give me a break! One little smørrebrød!"

> A Jew is trapped in a flood. He manages to reach the roof of his house and cries out, "God, please save me! I have faith in You!"
> Just then, a rowboat passes underneath, and the rower offers to have him jump in.
> "No," says the Jew, "I have faith in my God. I will wait for a sign from Him."
> Two more rowboats pass, and the Jew tells them the same thing. Finally, the water rises over the roof, and he drowns.
> He reaches the gates of heaven and cries out, "God, I have been a faithful, pious Jew. I asked you to save me, but you failed."
> "What are you talking about?" replies God. "I sent you three boats."

The following tale is based on an actual Talmudic passage:[1]

---

1. Babylonian Talmud, Baba Metsia 59b

Four rabbis are always arguing about the meaning of passages in the Torah. And always, three of them are on one side, and the same rabbi is on the other.

One day, as they argue yet again, the vote comes down the usual three to one. The habitual loser looks up to the heavens and cries, "Lord, I know I am right! Please give us a sign you agree with me!"

Suddenly, a peal of thunder shakes the air.

"You see?" says the supplicant.

"Just a natural occurrence," reply the other three.

"Lord," cries out the lone rabbi, "they do not believe this was a sign from you. Please give another sign."

A bolt of lightning crashes at their feet.

"Another natural occurrence," sniff the three.

"Please, Lord, give them an unambiguous sign you agree with me!"

A crack appears in the sky, a dazzling light appears in the crack, and the voice of the Lord says, "I agree. He is right."

The three rabbis turn to their colleague. "Okay, so now it's three to two."

A Jewish mountain climber is caught in a sudden avalanche. As he is swept down the mountain by the rushing snow, he manages to grab a branch. Hanging on for dear life, he casts his eyes heavenward and cries, "Lord, Lord, please save me!"

The sky opens, and a beam of blinding light appears. A voice from heaven is heard, "Trust in me. Let go of the branch."

The Jew again casts his eyes heavenward and asks, "Is there someone else up there I could talk to?"

A Chicago Jew drops to his knees in prayer. "Lord, I have but one request. Please let me win the Illinois lottery."

From heaven comes a voice: "It shall be done!"

The Jew checks the winners the next week ... and the week after ... and the week after that. No luck.

Again he drops to his knees: "Lord, you promised I would win the lottery. Why have you failed me?"

From heaven comes a voice: "Help me out. Buy a ticket!"

A Jew asks God, "Is it true that a million years is to you like one second?"

"Yes," comes a voice from Heaven.

"And is it also true that a million dollars is to you just like a penny?"

"Yes," again replies the heavenly voice.

"Lord," says the Jew, "please send me a penny."
"Just a second."

"Lord," implores a Jew, "if you send me a million dollars, I promise I will give half of it to the poor."
There is no answer.
"Okay, Lord," says the Jew. "You take care of the poor. Just send me my half-million."

The Satmar Rebbe, leader of one of the most fanatically pious sects in all of Judaism, dies and goes to heaven. At the pearly gates, a host of angels greets him. The Angel Gabriel steps forward.
"Rebbe, it is rare indeed that we have such an august personage as yourself join us. In your honor, there will be a reception and banquet!"
"A reception and banquet," muses the rebbe. "May I ask, who is the mazhgiekh?"[2]
Gabriel stares at him. "Rebbe, this is heaven. The Reboyne-sheloylem,[3] God himself is the mazhgiekh."
The rebbe says, "I'll have the fruit plate."

---

2. Supervisor of the food to make sure it is kosher
3. Master of the World

ZIONISM AND ISRAEL

The reestablishment of Jewish sovereignty after almost two millennia unsurprisingly gives rise to a new brand of humor. Many new brands in fact, including humor of the Zionist pioneers, Ashkenazic and Sephardic Israelis (as well as Israeli Arab and Palestinian Arab humor). Here are a few of my favorites:

> There are many stories about the lack of arms and equipment that plagued the Jews during Israel's War of Independence. One such tells of a new immigrant who volunteers for the just-born Israeli Navy. He signs up and requests a uniform.
> "Sorry, we don't have uniforms," the recruiting officer tells him.
> "How about a rifle or pistol?" asks the new recruit.
> "Sorry, we don't have any."
> As the recruit leaves the office, the enlistment officer stops him.
> "I forgot to ask. Can you swim?"
> "What!" exclaims the new recruit. "No boats either?"

A very popular theme is the almost, but not quite, success of Israel in achieving a western level of comfort, convenience, and, especially, orderliness.

> A Jew is asked whether he would rather be in American hell or Israeli hell.
> "What's the difference?"
> "No difference. In each, you are awakened daily at four in the morning, driven into a scalding hot shower, and then made to stand at strict attention for the rest of the day."
> "That's it?" says the Jew. "Then I choose the Israeli hell."
> "Why?"
> "Because, in the American hell, I'd be awakened daily at four in the morning, driven into a scalding hot shower, and then made to stand at strict attention for the rest of the day. In the Israeli hell, it might be daily. It might be five days out of seven. It might be every other day. It might be four in the morning. It might be four-thirty. It might be six. The shower might be scalding hot. It might just be pretty hot. It might be lukewarm. And I'd be

standing maybe all day, maybe a half-day, or maybe only a couple of hours. Who knows?"

In the 1960s, Israel produced an appalling cigarette called Silon. A group of Israeli tourists is given a tour of the Silon factory. The guide inadvertently opens the supply room, and the Israelis see a small pile of tobacco and an enormous pile of horse manure inside.

The embarrassed guide quickly shuts the door and says to the tourists, "I sincerely hope you won't tell anyone what you just saw."

"Tell anyone?" they reply. "We're going to tell everyone. We had no idea you used any tobacco."

A British airplane company keeps failing in its attempts to produce a jet that goes faster than sound. Every time the plane reaches Mach 1, the wings crack off.

Finally, they hire an Israeli engineer, who takes one look and says, "Drill holes along the wing, just where it's been cracking."

The British are aghast. By all rights, that should further weaken an already flawed construction. Nevertheless, they try it. Voilà! The plane not only achieves Mach 1, but Mach 2 without mishap.

"What engineering principle did you use to accomplish this?" they ask the Israeli.

"I don't know the principle," he replies. "What I do know is that, in my country, we have a special bread called matzoh, which has several rows of perforations. You can break that matzoh anywhere, but never along the perforations."

Actually, when I was living in Israel in the early 1960s, that joke was not about matzoh. It was about toilet paper.

An American Jewish couple visiting Israel are asked if they'd like to see the Tomb of the Unknown Soldier. They are taken to the tomb and read the inscription: "Mendl Goldfaden, Purveyor of Fine Furs."

"But how can he be the Unknown Soldier?" they ask.

"Oh," says the guide, "as a soldier, he was unknown. As a furrier, he was famous."

A story is told of the 1970s when American Secretary of State Henry Kissinger visited Israel during one of his ill-fated attempts at shuttle diplomacy.

He is taken to the Kotel[1] by Prime Minister Golda Meir, who tells him, according to tradition, if you pray at the Wall, your prayers will be answered. Kissinger decides to give it a try.

"I wish," says he, "Israel would relinquish all territories conquered in the Six-Day War as a sign of goodwill without expecting any quid pro quo from its Arab neighbors."

Says Golda, "You're talking to the wall."

Just before he died, David Ben Gurion was visited by the Angel of Death, who offered him the choice of heaven or hell.

"Let's have a look at both," says the former Israeli Prime Minister. So, the angel first takes him to heaven. It's pretty nice. It's quiet. Many people are sitting around studying, reading, or playing the harp, but it lacks the action and excitement Ben Gurion relishes.

"How about hell?" he asks. Down they go. Hell proves much more to his liking—speeches, political rallies, good food, and drink. All in all, it's a fun place.

Some months later when Ben Gurion dies and the Angel of Death asks him his choice, he does not hesitate at all. He points downward. So down he goes through the doors of hell, where he finds devils with pitchforks, people screaming, hot tar, fire, and brimstone. Not at all what he remembers.

"What happened?" he asks. "This place was much nicer last time I was here."

"Ah," replies the Angel of Death, "you were a tourist then. Now you're an immigrant."

The early twentieth-century Yiddish writer Sholem Asch, who wrote controversial novels about Jesus and Mary, had a reputation as a cheapskate. Legend has it that, in the 1920s, Asch was visiting the Sea of Galilee, near the locale of the Sermon on the Mount, and wanted to take a boat across to the other side. When the oarsman quoted him the price of the ride, Asch reputedly said, "No wonder Jesus walked!"

A thief holds up a bank in Tel Aviv. He escapes with 5,000 shekels in cash and 20,000 in pledges.

---

1. The Western Wall, the only remaining wall of the Jewish Temple, destroyed by the Romans in 70 CE

The early (and not so early) Zionist rejection of Diaspora Judaism as a culture of exile has been a source of great controversy ... and laughter.

> An elderly Israeli is speaking to her granddaughter in Yiddish. Another passenger upbraids her, "Speak Hebrew! Why are you speaking to her in Yiddish?"
> Grandma replies, "I don't want her to forget she's a Jew."

To be a shaliakh, an emissary from Israel to Jewish communities in the Diaspora, was considered a plum appointment.

> The story is told of a kibbutz[2] with a remarkable bull. He works hard pulling the plow all day and sires many calves. His fame reaches an African country with no diplomatic relations with Israel. The African nation agrees to establish relations, if they can have the bull on loan for a half year. The Israeli government agrees, and the kibbutz ships the bull to Africa.
> Three weeks later, there comes an irate letter from the African country. The Israelis have tricked them. The bull is useless. Israel quickly dispatches a kibbutznik[3] to see what's gone wrong. When the kibbutznik arrives, it is immediately obvious what the problem is. Instead of working, the bull is lounging in the grass, flirting with a herd of cows.
> "What gives?" the kibbutznik asks the bull. "At home, you were industrious and responsible. Here, you're a lazy good-for-nothing."
> "Ah," says the bull. "At home, I was a kibbutznik. Here I'm a shaliakh."

American Jewish youth have been kibbutz volunteers since Israel was established. So, of course, there must be a joke about them.

> An American volunteer is staffing the kibbutz office one evening when the phone rings.
> "Shalom," says the voice, "I'm stuck in Tel Aviv at a meeting and won't get back to the kibbutz until morning. Will you please go to my cabin, the fifth one to the left of the dining hall, and let my wife know?"
> "Sure," says the volunteer, "hold the line."
> Five minutes later, the volunteer gets back on the phone and says, "There's a problem. I went to your cabin and knocked, and no one answered. I went around the back, looked in the window, and saw a couple making love. What should I do?"

---

2. Israeli communal farm
3. Member of the kibbutz

"Here's what you do," replies the voice. "Go back to the cabin. On the porch is my old army knapsack. Open it, and you'll find my pistol. Go around to the window, and shoot my wife and her lover. Then take the gun and throw it into the river just on the side of the cabin."

"Okay, hold the phone," says the volunteer.

Five minutes later, the volunteer gets back on the phone and says, "There's a problem. I went to your cabin, found the knapsack, took the pistol, and shot your wife and her lover. Then I went to throw the gun in the river, but I can't seem to find the river."

There's a long silence. Then the voice says, "What kibbutz is this?"

A Jewish lady embarks on a British Airlines flight from Miami to Israel. She has a large box under her arm.

"Madam," says the flight attendant, "you have to check that in the baggage."

"But that's my dog," says the lady.

"Nevertheless," says the attendant, "it's too large for the plane. We'll put it in the hold, and I assure you it will be fine."

When the plane stops in London, the attendant goes down into the hold to check on the animal. She opens the box and sees a cocker spaniel—dead. In a frenzy, she asks her coworkers what she should do.

"Not a problem," they tell her. "Just down the road, there's a nice kennel. No doubt, you can find an identical dog." Which she does. She disposes of the dead beast and places the live one in the box.

Upon landing in Israel, the attendant gives the lady the box. She opens it, and the dog is wagging its tail in joy.

"That's not my dog!" cries the lady.

"What do you mean?" says the attendant. "How can you say it's not your dog?"

"My dog was dead. I was taking it to Israel to bury it!"

An Israeli soldier stationed on the Golan Heights is continually receiving medals of valor and three-day passes for capturing Syrian tanks. One of his comrades asks him how he manages this trick.

"Not so hard," replies the soldier. "I drive one of our tanks across the lines and find a Syrian tank driver who also wants a three-day pass. So we exchange tanks."

Two guys meet on the golf course of a Jewish country club.

"So what do you do when you're not playing golf?" asks the first.

"I'm the club rabbi," says the second and proceeds to trounce his new partner in golf.

The trouncee licks his wounds, goes home, and decides he needs a trip to Israel. He winds up at a posh club in Caesarea, right on the water, in view of Tel Aviv. As he walks out onto the golf course, who does he see, but his former golfing partner.

"Don't tell me you're the rabbi of this club, too."

"No," replies the rabbi. "Here, I'm the golf pro."

Chaim, just arrived from Tel Aviv on a business trip to Amsterdam, hails a cab and asks to be taken to a certain address. It turns out to be in the famous red-light district. Although somewhat surprised, Chaim enters the bordello and asks the madam if she knows an Israeli named Rivka Harel.

"Yes," she says, "Rivka is one of our best girls. Would you like her services?"

"Sure," says Chaim.

The assignation is arranged. As price is discussed, Chaim says, "Look, I have 1,000 Israeli shekels. What can I get for that?"

"Quite a bit," says Rivka. She then proceeds to show him—to his prolonged delight.

After several pleasurable hours, Chaim dresses to leave. Rivka says, "So where in Israel are you from?"

"Tel Aviv," he replies.

"So am I," she says, "What street?"

"Agranot," he replies.

"That's my parents' street! What number?" asks Rivka excitedly.

"Twenty-seven," replies Chaim.

"But that's the very building where they live! You must know them!"

"Indeed I do," says Chaim. "Here's the 1,000 shekels they asked me to give you."

Israel has continued replying "no comment" to questions about its nuclear capability.

The story is told of an Arab counterpart asking the foreign minister if Israel might authorize a public tour of the secret facility in the Negev desert. He promptly refuses.

"But why? Wouldn't it be a sign of goodwill to show us what you have?" asked the Arab diplomat. "What risk would you be taking?"

"Maybe," replied the foreign minister, "you'll discover we have nothing."

A newly arrived Russian immigrant opens a bank account and withdraws his first fifty shekels. Eager to show off his command of Hebrew, he counts out the money in a loud voice, "Ekhad, shtayim, shalosh …"

Completing the count, he starts again.

The bank clerk, pretty irritated by now, asks, "What's the matter? Didn't I give you the right amount?"

"Yes," sniffs the immigrant, "but just barely."

Finally, a story demonstrating the Jewish adage, "We are all one."

Two American Jews decide to sample Tel Aviv nightlife. They go to a café, where an Israeli comic is entertaining an appreciative crowd in Hebrew, which neither of the Americans can speak. One of the Americans laughs uproariously with the audience.

"What are you laughing at?" asks his colleague. "You don't understand Hebrew."

"So what?" is the reply. "I trust these people!"

SEX

Jewish jokes about sex play off two stereotypes. The first is that Jews are not particularly sexy. (Take a look at TV's Jewish sitcom characters, and you'll see what I mean.) The second is that, contrary to the evidence of our own existence, our grandparents and people their age would never do such a thing. Jewish sexual humor happily exploits both of these. Also, many of these stories take place in Miami, the only place where a demographic snapshot would force one to conclude that people are born Cuban and die Jewish.

> Abe Schwartz, well into middle age, takes a young bride. The marriage seems to be going well, except for one thing. Mrs. Schwartz, in spite of all their efforts, seems unable to get pregnant. Abe goes to the doctor, who advises him, "Mr. Schwartz, I advise you to take in a boarder."
> "And you think that'll help?"
> "Trust me," says the doctor. "It'll help."
> Six months later, Abe returns to the doctor, wreathed in smiles. "You were right! My wife is pregnant!"
> "Ah," says the doctor, "You followed my advice and took in a boarder?"
> "Yeh," says Abe, "she's pregnant, too."

> A priest of a Miami church hears someone come into the confessional. He asks the penitent for his confession.
> "Vell," says an elderly voice, "I'm eighty-two years old. I vas coming yesterday out of de supermarket mit my peckeges, ven, boomp! I'm knocked over from behind. I pick myself up, and der's a beautiful young blonde apologizing and helping me pick up my groceries. Suddenly, she says to me 'You're pretty cute.' Vun ting leads to anodder, and, de next ting you know, ve're over at my place—doing it! And ve did it four times!"
> The priest interrupts this discourse. "This is all very interesting, but it seems to me that you are not a member of my church or even a Catholic. Why are you telling me this?"
> "Telling you? I'm telling everyvun!"

Abie and Becky have been lovers ever since they met in the Miami Senior Citizens' Center. Each evening, he makes his way over to her apartment for a little hanky-panky. One night, he's late. Becky begins worrying.

A half hour later, there's a knock on the door. It's Abie, safe and sound.

"What happened?" asks Becky. "I was worried."

"Oh," says Abie, "on my way here, I passed a dark alley, and I heard some young fellas boasting, 'I'll bet you fifty dollars mine is bigger than yours!' So I went into the alley and asked if I could get a piece of the action. They said sure, so here I am. And here's the fifty dollars."

"Abie," says Becky, "you took your whole thing out in an alley?"

"Nah," says Abie, "not the whole thing. Just enough to win the bet."

Levine and Feinberg are sitting on their usual Miami park bench, making their usual bets.

"I'll bet you two dollars the next plane to fly overhead is a 747."

"I'll bet you three dollars the next girl to walk by is a natural blonde."

Finally, Levine says to Feinberg, "How about a real bet? I'll bet you $1,000 that soft is by me longer than is hard by you."

"Soft is by you longer than is hard by me?" says Feinberg. "You got a bet! So how long is soft by you?"

"Since 1956."

(Note: this ingenious joke works because of the ambiguity introduced by Yiddish syntax used in English.)

A Miami hooker sidles up to old Mr. Cohen and murmurs in a sultry voice, "For $200, I'll do anything you want."

He reaches into his pocket, hands her the $200, and says, "Paint my house."

Mollie and Sollie are residents of the same senior citizens' home. One day, Mollie says to Sollie, "I'll bet I can guess your age."

"Oh yeah," says Sollie. "How?"

"Come back to my place, and I'll show you," says Mollie.

They go to her room, and she tells Sollie to drop his shorts.

"What!" he cries.

"It's necessary in order for me to guess," Mollie assures him. So, he drops his shorts. Mollie fondles his privates for a couple of minutes and finally announces, "You're ninety-two."

"Amazing!" says Sollie. "How did you know?"

"You told me yesterday."

A young guy decides to get the quintessential Miami suntan. For a week, he lies on the beach in the briefest bikini trunks. The last day before he leaves, he decides he wants to perfect his tan. He goes out to the beach at sunup, finds a secluded spot, takes off his bathing suit, and buries himself in the sand. Only the bathing suit area is exposed to the sun. Unfortunately, he falls asleep.

At 10:30, Mrs. Cohen and Mrs. Klein are walking along the beach and stumble upon the secluded spot.

"Will you look at that!" exclaims Mrs. Cohen.

"Yeh," says Mrs. Klein. "Fifty years ago when I really needed it, I couldn't find it anywhere. Now that I don't care anymore, it's growing wild!"

An elderly couple present themselves at the office of a Florida gerontologist.

"Doctor, we have a problem. We're not sure we remember how to have sex. Would you mind giving us a consultation?"

"What do you mean?" asks the young doctor.

"Well, can we just try to do it on your examination table and you tell us if it's right?"

The dubious physician agrees. After all, what could it hurt? So they go at it, and he watches.

"Looks fine to me," he says. "That will be fifty dollars for an office visit."

They pay him and leave.

Next week, they're back again with the same request. They just aren't sure they aren't forgetting how to do it in the interim—what with short-term memory loss. So the doctor consents again.

By the fifth week, however, he's getting a little suspicious.

"Okay," he confronts them. "You do it fine. Why do you keep coming? It's costing you fifty bucks every time."

The couple blushes and replies, "It's like this. We're married to other people. If we sneak off to the Hotel Fontainebleau, we might be recognized. Anyway, a room is $200. Here it's safe, it only costs us fifty, and we get eighty percent back from Medicare."

Newly arrived in Miami, Mrs. Shulman is invited to join a mahjong club. At the first meeting, the other ladies explain the rules of the club, "First of all, no talk about money. Thank God, we're all comfortable. No need to compare incomes. Second, no talk about children. Thank God, we all have wonderful kids, who have good lives and produce darling grandchildren. No need to bore each other with the details. And finally, no talk about sex. Because what was—was!"

The widow Bernstein marries the widower Feldman. On their honeymoon, she explains to him what her expectations are.
"Mr. Bernstein was a very generous husband. Every year, he took me on a cruise."
"Fine," says Mr. Feldman. "I'm not a poor man. You want a cruise every year? You got it!"
"Mr. Bernstein," says his widow, "also liked to give me gifts. Every six months, I got either a car or a fur."
"Fine," agrees the new spouse, "a fur or a car, twice a year."
"And last but not least," says the new Mrs. Feldman, "Mr. Bernstein understood my womanly needs. I expect sex seven nights a week."
"No problem," replies Mr. Feldman. "Put me down for Tuesday."

This story is best told aloud:

Poor Morris is put in a convalescent home after major surgery. His poker buddies see he's really depressed, so they chip in and rent him a hooker for an evening. Morris is sitting in his room when his door opens and in comes a beautiful woman in a raincoat.
"What do you want?" asks Morris.
She opens her coat and is naked underneath. "Special for you," she purrs, "super sex."
Morris replies, "I'll have the soup."

"Sadie," asks Minnie, "tell me, do you and Sam have mutual orgasm?"
Sadie thinks for a minute and says, "No, I think we have State Farm."

Mr. Siegelboym is having a funny feeling in his loins. He goes to the doctor, who tells him, "Mr. Siegelboym, I'll need a sperm sample. Here's a bottle. Take it home, do what you need to do, and bring it back tomorrow."
Siegelboym returns the next day with the jar still empty.
"Doctor, my wife and I tried everything. First my hand. Then her hand. Then her mouth. But nothing worked. We just can't get the lid off!"

A middle-aged couple meets in the Catskills. It turns out he's a widower of some years, and she lost her husband a year ago. This is the first relationship for either of them. One thing leads to another, and they find themselves back in her cabin. After some pleasant preliminaries, he undresses her and attempts to continue the process.

"No, stop!" she cries. "You may touch me and kiss me wherever you like, but I'm still in mourning for my late husband. You cannot enter me."

He reluctantly settles for this, but tries again the next night—and receives the same answer. "I'm still in mourning for my late husband. You cannot enter me."

After a week of this, he visits her cabin again. When they undress this time, she notices he's wearing a jet-black condom.

"What in the world is that for?" she asks.

He answers, "I'm going to pay a shiva call."[1]

Sal and Angie Tortellini retire from the Bronx to Florida, where they become friends with Sam and Essie Tabachnik. One day, Sal and Angie ask Sam and Sadie how they manage to get to sleep every night.

"Well," reply the Tabachniks, "after we shower, we get into bed, we hug, we cuddle, we fondle a little, and then we sing Yiddish songs until we fall asleep in each other's arms."

The Tortellinis listen carefully and head home for the evening. The next day, the foursome is together, and Sam and Sadie ask Sal and Angie how it went.

"To tell you the truth," reply the Tortellinis, "not as well as we expected. We showered, we got into bed, we hugged, we cuddled, and we fondled. But we didn't know any Yiddish songs, so we just had to screw ourselves to sleep."

A little brother says to his sister, "Let's play Mommy and Daddy."

"How do we do that?" she asks.

"It's easy," replies her brother. "We go into their bedroom. We lock the door. Then we get all naked and into bed. We pull the covers over ourselves. Then we turn out the light."

"And then?"

"Then we talk Yiddish, so the children won't understand."

---

1. Condolence call

FAMILY

There are probably more Jewish mother jokes than there are Jewish mothers. (How many Jewish mothers does it take to screw in a light bulb? None. "I'll just sit here in the dark.") There are also Jewish father jokes, Jewish son jokes, and Jewish daughter jokes. Some of these fall well into the category of nasty and self-hating. I'm thinking particularly of Jewish American Princess jokes. They simply reiterate bigoted stereotypes about Jewish materialism and love of money and encourage Jewish men and women to hold each other in contempt as marriage partners. (Who are TV Jews always married to?) So excuse me, I'll take a pass. None of them here.

Much more interesting are the authentic jokes (some of them also nasty) that Jews have told and tell about family members. Are there particular character traits? Is the Jewish mother always the Typhoid Mary of guilt? Is the Jewish father always constipated? Not so far as I can tell. The stories are multidimensional, just like the people they portray.

> Marvin Goldblatt calls his mother from the University of Iowa. "Mama, I have wonderful news! I'm getting married!"
> "So what's her name?" asks Mrs. Goldblatt.
> "Christine Peterson," says Marvin, not without some trepidation.
> "Mmm ...," replies Mama, calmly. "And when and where shall the nuptials take place?"
> "We're coming to New York next week to find a nondenominational house of worship. Christine's parents are coming with us. Do you think you and Papa could put us all up for the weekend?"
> "Sure, no problem," says Mrs. Goldblatt. "The Petersons can stay in our bedroom. You can stay in yours. Your lovely bride can take the guest room, and Papa will sleep on the living room couch."
> "But what about you, Mama?"
> "Oh, that's not a problem," says Mrs. Goldblatt. "As soon as you hang up, I'm throwing myself out the window."

Howie Solomon calls his mother from North Dakota State University.

"Mama, I have wonderful news! I got married!"

"Oh? To whom, may I ask?" says Mama.

"She's a Native American," replies Howie. "And you'll meet her and her family tomorrow. We're flying to New York."

The next day, Mrs. Solomon's bell rings. She opens the door to see Howie, together with his bride and two men, all in their native garb.

"Mama, I'd like you to meet my wife, Running Deer; my father-in-law, Stalking Bear; and my brother-in-law, Soaring Eagle."

"Very pleased to make your acquaintance," says Mrs. Solomon. "I'm Howard's mother, Sitting Shiva."[1]

Morris is very proud of his son Sheldon, the great surgeon. In fact, when Morris needs a serious operation, he asks Sheldon to perform the surgery.

"Pop, that's a really bad idea."

Morris insists either Sheldon do it or he won't have the surgery. Sheldon reluctantly agrees.

Just as the anesthetist is about to administer the Pentothal, Morris looks up at Sheldon and says, "If anything goes wrong, Mama is coming to live with you and your wife."

Gentiles who convert to Judaism are welcomed, but Jews often view them with bemusement. Why would anyone do such a thing? Added to this is the typically American phenomenon that the converted partner in a marriage, especially if female, often winds up more knowledgeable about and committed to Judaism than her Jewish-born spouse.

His father sends young Herbert Goldstein off to college with one piece of advice. "Don't marry a shikse."

Nevertheless, this is America, and Herbert meets and falls in love with the lovely Harriet Vanderbosch. Harriet, for her part, becomes enamored not just of Herbert, but of Judaism. She studies and undergoes conversion. The couple is married by a rabbi, according to the Laws of Moses and Israel, and sets up house. Herbert, now an MBA, joins his father in the wholesale dry goods business.

One evening, Pop calls Herbert at home and tells him, "Next Saturday, we gotta do inventory. Come in at 8:30 AM, and we'll work through the day."

---

1. Observing the mourning period after the death of a relative; a popular threat of Jewish parents to children who considered marrying out of the fold.

"Listen, Pop, I'm sorry," says Herbert. "Harriet's made it a family tradition to keep the Sabbath strictly according to Jewish Law, so I can't work Saturdays."

"You see?" shouts Pop. "I told you not to marry a shikse!"

Young Adam Shapiro has worked hard at his acting craft. He finally lands a role in an off-Broadway play. He comes home to share the good news with his parents.

"So what's the part?" asks Morris Shapiro.

"Actually, Dad, I play the role of a Jewish father."

Morris looks disappointed.

"What's the matter?" asks Adam.

"I was hoping it would be a speaking part."

The first American Jewish president calls his mother. "Mom, we're celebrating Rosh Hashonah next week in the White House. Won't you please join us?"

"Ach, it's too hard. A long shlep from Miami to Washington. And what would I eat? Where would I sleep?"

"Mom, please," begs the president, "I can arrange everything. A limousine will take you to a private jet, and another limo will bring you here. I've ordered strictly kosher food and purchased a separate set of dishes. And you'll have the entire East Wing to yourself."

"I'll call you back in a few days and let you know," says Mama.

Four days later, she calls back. "So okay, I'll come," she grudgingly consents. On Rosh Hashonah, she's sitting on the White House Lawn listening to her son make a speech about the beauty of the Jewish holidays.

A reporter turns to her and says, "You must be so proud to be here."

"It's okay," admits Mama, "but I can't understand why I didn't get an invitation this year from my other son, the doctor."

"Hello, Mama," cries a voice on the phone. "You've got to come over and help me. I'm at my wits' end! Mr. Bigshot is off playing golf with his buddies, leaving me with all the housework and the two kids, both of whom are throwing up and screaming. I can't stand it any more. I'm just gonna kill myself!"

"Darling, don't worry," comes the reply. "I can be there in fifteen minutes. You'll relax. I'll do a little vacuuming, make a nice lunch, get my darling grandchildren down for their naps, and then we can sit quiet and have a nice cup of tea. You'll tell me all your troubles."

"Oh, Mama, I knew I could count on you! Stevie and Jennifer will be so happy to see their grandma."

"Who? My grandchildren are Bobbie and Erin. You must have the wrong number."

There's silence at the other end. Then a plaintive voice says, "Does this mean you're not coming?"

Two Jewish ladies meet on a cruise. One says to the other, "That's a beautiful ring you're wearing."

"Thank you. This is a very famous diamond, like the Hope Diamond or the Star of India. This is the Plotkin Diamond. Unfortunately, it comes with a curse."

"What sort of curse?"

"Mr. Plotkin."

A man rushes into his psychiatrist's office as soon as it opens. "Oh, doctor, thanks for agreeing to see me so early. I'm sorry I woke you, but I had the most awful dream. I dreamed my mother was coming at me. Her arms were reaching out to grab me. Suddenly, her faced changed into yours! I screamed and woke up in a cold sweat. So I called you, grabbed a shower and a Coke, and rushed down here. What do you think it means?"

"A Coke?" says the psychiatrist. "That you call a breakfast?"

Papa calls up his married son and daughter one August day. "Listen, I've decided to divorce your mother."

"What?" shriek the children. "Why? You and Mama always seemed so happy together."

"Nevertheless, I just don't love her anymore, and I've decided to end the marriage. Next month is Rosh Hashonah. That's the last holiday we'll celebrate together. Right after the holiday dinner, I'm going to ask her for a divorce."

"Oh, Papa, she'll be shattered! The least we can do is fly in and be there when you announce it."

"Okay," says Papa, "See you then." He hangs up the phone, turns to Mama, and says, "Well, that worked. What'll we tell them to get them here next Pesakh?"

Here's a subtle little number, the Gentile mother joke:

A Gentile mother calls her son on Sunday morning and says, "Darling, I'm so glad you can come for dinner. I spent all day yesterday preparing your favorites—roast pork with dressing; mashed potatoes; a green bean, mushroom, and fried onion casserole; and, of course, a nice apple pie."

"Mom," says the son, "I'm really sorry. Something's come up, and I just won't be able to make it."

"That's okay. No problem."

(Get it?)

In the Old Country, marriages among Jews from different villages were sometimes arranged by mail. Bride and groom never met until the engagement was sealed.

One such groom travels from his village to the village of his intended. When he gets off the train, he sees—not one—but two young women with their mothers. There was a mix-up somewhere, and each claims him as her intended spouse.

The dispute escalates until all parties are brought before the Bet Din, the rabbinical court. The court hears the claims of both parties. The chief rabbi finally decrees, "We shall take the young man and cut him in half, and you can each have a part of him."

One of the mothers shrieks in horror.

The other says, "It seems like a fine solution."

The rabbi points at her and says, "That's the real mother-in-law."

Sammie comes to his father and asks for an increase in his allowance.

"And, if I increase it, then what?"

"Then I'll save it up to buy a bike."

"And, with a bike, then what?"

"Then I'll be able to have a paper route and earn even more money."

"And, with more money, then what?"

"Then I'll gain business experience, which will help me get an MBA when I grow up."

"And, with an MBA, then what?"

"Then I'll be able to open my own business."

"And, with your own business, then what?"

"Then I'll be able to make a good living, find a nice wife, and settle down."

"And then what?"

"Then I'll be happy!"

"And, if you're happy, so then what?"

Two middle-aged Jewish ladies are getting acquainted at the Jewish community center.

"So what do your children do?" asks the one.
"I don't have children," replies the other.
"Really? What do you do for tsores?"[2]

Abe is on his deathbed. Sadie, his wife of sixty years, is at his side.
"Sadie," he murmurs, "remember how we grew up in Poland? All those anti-Semites …"
"Yes, Abe. I was with you through those times."
"And the war? The ghetto, the concentration camp?"
"Yes, Abe, we were together."
"And immigrating to America? I thought the ship would capsize. I was so sick."
"Yes, darling, I was with you."
"And miserable jobs and the years I went bankrupt?"
"Yes, darling, I was there with you through it all."
"And, now this, my final illness."
"And here I am, still at your side, my dear Abie."
"You know, Sadie," says Abe, "with you I never had any mazel."[3]

Mollie and Morrie are taking a bus tour of New York City.
"This is the famous Vanderbilt Mansion," says the guide.
"Cornelius Vanderbilt?" asks Morrie.
"No," replies the guide, "William Vanderbilt."
They go further and stop at another beautiful building.
"And this is the Astor Mansion," says the guide.
"John Jacob Astor?" asks Morrie.
"No, Vincent Astor," says the guide.
Finally, the bus stops in from of a beautiful church.
"And this is the famous Christ Church," says the guide.
Mollie grabs Morrie's arm and mutters, "Please. Don't ask."

Wealthy industrialist and former member of Knesset, Yigal Even-Zohar is celebrating his fiftieth wedding anniversary with his lovely wife Pnina in their sumptuously appointed Tel Aviv home. After the last guests leave, Yigal turns to Pnina and says, "Darling, we've been married fifty years. Tell me, have you ever been unfaithful?"

---

2. Woes; troubles
3. Luck

Pnina blushes and says, "I can't lie to you, my darling. Yes. Three times. But only for your own good."

"My own good? What do you mean?"

"You remember," says Pnina, "when we first arrived in Israel after the war, and they put us in those terrible barracks? And how the fellow from Immigrant Absorption suddenly came a few days later and moved us to a nice apartment? Well, that was the first time … with him."

"And the second time?"

"You remember when you needed a few thousand shekels to start your business and the bank refused? Then suddenly they gave you the loan? Well, I went to the manager of the bank. That was the second time."

"And the third time?" asks Yigal.

"You remember when you were running for Knesset and you were only short fourteen votes?"

Part Two
Laughing Outward

Thus far, we have been laughing inward, dealing with humor directed by Jews at their own communities. Now let us turn to laughing outward, humor directed at the non-Jewish world. How do Jews respond to societies in which we are a minority? One thing we do is make jokes. What kind? It depends. From the beginning of the Exile, after the Roman destruction of the Second Temple in 70 CE, Jews have found themselves in societies that were alternately tolerant and oppressive. The same society was sometimes both. Unfortunately, the oppressive has dominated the tolerant over the last two millennia. Thus, jokes about anti-Semitism abound. Only lately, mostly in America, does a new kind of humor arise—what we might call dialogue humor, the friendly competition between Jews and Gentiles.

EUROPEAN JEWISH HUMOR

In this section, we deal predominantly with the jokes Jews have invented about their oppression and their oppressors. It's not that the European experience was uniformly negative. However, the Laughing Inward category pretty much covered that which was positive. By and large, throughout the Jews' two-millennia sojourn in Europe, laughing outward has been an outlet against persecution and humiliation.

DISPUTATIONS

Even in the worst times, perhaps even more so in those times, Jews mocked their enemies. In the Middle Ages, for example, Christian attempts to convert the Jews were constant and often violent. Sometimes, they took the form of the feared disputation, in which a Christian would challenge the Jews to a discussion about the relative merits of the two religions. The stakes were often death or banishment for the whole community. The Jews were, of course, in a terrible spot. They had to find a way to win—without insulting the authorities and thereby subjecting themselves to even more violence. In reality, this was rarely possible. But in humor ...

> A priest challenges the local Jewish community to produce a scholar to debate him on religion. The rules: The debate has to be nonverbal. The stakes: if the Jews lose, they have to give up their homes and leave the country within three days.
> Who among them will undertake the awesome burden of this challenge? Yossele the water carrier, a simple man with a mere two years of kheder[1] education, volunteers. The community is amazed and aghast, but since no one else steps forward ...
> Yossele presents himself at the appointed time in the town square. The priest goes first. He waves his arms in an arc. Yossele points to the ground. The priest puts up three fingers. Yossele raises one. The priest takes out a wafer, eats it, and washes it down with some wine. Yossele takes out an apple and bites into it.
> The priest turns to the crowd and says, "As much as I hate to admit it, this Jew has beaten me. We shall leave you alone."
> With that, he marches off with his entourage. His followers ask him, "What was the debate? How did the Jew beat you?"
> The priest replies, "I waved my arms to signify the arch of the heavens above was the true realm of the Lord. He reminded me the Lord brought us out

---

1. Elementary school for Jewish boys, starting at age three

from the earth and shall return us there. I proclaimed the sanctity of the Holy Trinity. He reminded me they are all manifestations of the one God. I spoke of the sacrifice of Christ, his body, and blood incarnate in the Eucharist. The Jew reminded me it was the original sin of Adam and Eve that made Christ's sacrifice necessary. How can one not stand in awe of such theological genius?"

Meanwhile, the Jews are questioning Yossele about what had transpired.

"I'm not sure," he replies. "He waved his arms to tell me we all have to leave, so I pointed at the ground to tell him we're staying right here. He told me we had three days to prepare for exile, so I told him not one of us was going. He took out his lunch, so I took out mine."

A priest challenges the local Jewish community to produce a scholar to debate him on the Hebrew language. The rules: The contestants will put their heads on a chopping block. The first one who doesn't know the answer to a question posed by the other will have his head summarily cut off by a waiting executioner. But the priest is magnanimous as well as confident. He will let the Jew ask the first question.

Who among them will undertake the awesome burden of this challenge? Yossele the water carrier, a simple man with a mere two years of kheder education, volunteers. The community is amazed and aghast, but since no one else steps forward …

Yossele presents himself at the appointed time in the town square. He and the priest put their heads on adjacent blocks. The executioner raises his axe. The priest motions Yossele to begin.

"What," asks Yossele, "is the meaning of the Hebrew phrase 'Eyneyni yoydea?'"

The priest answers, correctly, "I don't know."

Snick! Down comes the axe, and the contest is over.

The Jews are jubilant. They hold a big feast in honor of Yossele and their own salvation. As the revelry gets underway, the town elders approach Yossele to compliment him on his genius in choosing such a clever question.

"What's the big deal?" demurs Yossele. "When I was a boy in kheder, I had a melamed who was the most brilliant teacher I have ever seen. One day, we came across the words 'Eyneyni yoydea.' I asked my melamed what they meant. He replied 'I don't know.' If such a brilliant man as my melamed didn't know, you think that priest could have known?"

CZARIST RUSSIA

"Di velt iz kaylekhdik" (The world is round) goes the Yiddish expression, which means the political far left is indistinguishable from the far right, certainly with regard to the Jews. Czarist Russia and its successor, the Soviet Union, vied for which was more anti-Semitic. Each produced its own form of Jewish humor.

> In nineteenth-century Czarist Russia, a plan was devised to convert the Jews. The first step was to lure them away from their own schools. Special schools were opened with Jewish students and Jewish teachers, but the school inspectors were Russians ... and usually anti-Semites.
> One such visits a school, marches into the math class, pushes aside the teacher, and announces, "You Jews think you're so smart? Here's a problem for you: A train is traveling a distance of 750 verst from Town A to Town B. The train has twenty-five cars. In each car are eighteen passengers. How old am I?"
> Silence reigns. Then a hand goes up in the back.
> "You're forty-eight," answers a young student.
> The inspector is amazed. "How did you know?"
> "Simple arithmetic," says the student. "In our shtetl, there's a guy who's twenty-four. And he's half-meshuge."

During the days of the czar, Jews were restricted to living in what was called the Pale of Settlement. Only those few with specially needed trades could live in the cities. Others required a special pass that was difficult to obtain, even to visit relatives there. Some took their chances and visited without a pass. The story is told of two brothers, one with permission to live in Moscow and the other visiting him on the sly. They are taking an after-dinner stroll when they suddenly see a policeman beginning to follow them.

> The resident says to his brother, "I'll run away. The policeman will chase me. When he loses sight of you, just disappear and make your way out of the city."

All goes as planned. The legal brother starts running. The policeman chases him, shouting, "Stop, Jew!" The other brother steals away to safety.

When the resident sees his brother is safe, he stops. The policeman grabs him by the collar.

"Ha, Jew, I caught you! You're here without a pass!"

"Not at all," replies the Jew, producing his pass.

"But then why were you running?" asks the policeman.

"My doctor told me it's good for my health to run every evening after dinner."

"But," persists the policeman, "why didn't you stop when you saw me running after you?"

"I assumed you had the same doctor."

A Jew is sitting on a train when a Russian general with a large German shepherd comes into his car. Not at all pleased to be sharing a compartment with a Jew, the general decides to insult him. He turns to the dog and says, "Yitskhak, sit! Yitskhak, roll over! Yitskhak, speak!"

The Jew, far from taking umbrage, shakes his head, "Oy, such a shame for the dog."

"What's a shame?" asks the general.

"That the dog has a Jewish name."

"Why is that a shame?"

"Because otherwise," says the Jew, "he could be a general."

Talking about the Russian military, a particularly horrible practice in the nineteenth century was the virtual kidnapping of so-called cantonists, young Jewish boys forcibly inducted into the czar's army for twenty-five years. Many lost contact with their family and their faith. When the khappers, the grabbers, were sighted, the cry went out. All the young boys in the shtetl were hidden.

As the khappers are heading into a shtetl, the melamed takes all of the young boys into a cellar hidden by a trapdoor. There they sit in the dark, scarcely daring to breathe. Suddenly, they hear the door above slam open and then shut. Footsteps rush over to the trapdoor. A voice cries out in Yiddish, "Open up! Let an old Jew in! The khappers are coming!"

"What are you worried about?" calls up the melamed. "You're not a young boy. You're an old man."

"Oh?" replies the voice. "And generals they don't need?"

A Jew falls into the Volga River.

"Help!" he cries. "Help!"
The passing policemen ignore his cries.
Finally, with his last breath, he shouts, "Down with the czar!"
With which, they jump in, pull him out, and arrest him.

A Jew is walking down the streets of Moscow when the czar's carriage drives by. The czar, in a Jew-baiting mood, orders his driver to stop. He dismounts and tells the Jew, "Get down in the gutter behind my horses, and eat what you find there."
The poor Jew complies. When he's finally allowed to rise, he is so humiliated that he takes the chance of his life. He overpowers the driver, wrests his pistol from him, points it at the czar, and says, "Now you get down behind your horses and eat what's there." The czar complies.
After he finishes, the Jew, holding them at bay, disappears into an alley and runs off home.
When he arrives, his wife asks, "Anything interesting happen today?"
"You'll never guess who I had lunch with."

Two Jewish revolutionaries are in front of a Russian firing squad. The captain offers the first Jew a blindfold, which he gratefully accepts. The captain offers the same to the second Jew, who spits in his face and shouts out, "Down with the czar!"
His comrade turns to him and says, "Please, we're in enough trouble already."

A Jewish dentist decides to emigrate from Czarist Russia. But he doesn't want to leave, like most of his coreligionists, penniless. He needs to find a way to take his fortune, such as it is, with him. He turns all of his worldly goods into gold. From which, he can make seven sets of false teeth. He packs these in his bag and heads for the border, where he is, of course, stopped by the guards, who find the teeth.
"What do you need so many sets of gold teeth for?" they ask.
"I'm a very religious Jew," replies the dentist. "One set is for when I eat meat. One is for dairy, and one is for pareve."[1]
"But what about the other sets?" persist the guards.
"You know," says the Jew, "for our Passover holiday, we cannot use the same dishes. Because I am very strict in observance, I have one set of teeth for Passover meat, one for dairy, and the third for pareve."

---

1. Neither meat nor dairy, for example, vegetables or fish. Pronounced PAH-reh-veh.

"That's six. What's the seventh set for?"
"Every once in a while," replies the dentist, "I get such a craving for pork."

WESTERN EUROPE

Western European Jews had their own anti-anti-Semitic humor:

> In the seventeenth century, a Danish Jew is walking down the streets of Copenhagen when some boys begin throwing clods of mud at him. He turns, walks over to the boys, and gives them each a ten-øre[1] piece.
> This goes on for a week. At the end of the week, the boys throw the mud again. The Jew turns to them and says, "I'm sorry, but I've run out of change."
> So they stop.

There's a variant of this told by East European Jews:

> A peasant stops a Jew on the street and gives him a smack in the face.
> "Thank you," says the Jew and gives the peasant twenty kopecks.
> "What's that for?" asks the puzzled peasant.
> "It's part of our tradition that, on Purim, the holiday we celebrate today, we are honored to be smacked by our Gentile neighbors and are required to reward them. In fact, you would do well to go to the rich end of town and do the same to Baron de Hirsch."
> The peasant hurries to the de Hirsch mansion, knocks on the door, asks to see the baron, and proceeds to smack him in the face. The baron's servants duly proceed to beat the living daylights out of the peasant and throw him into the ditch.
> He picks himself up and hobbles off, muttering, "Damn Jews. Don't even know their own customs."

You probably know the famous legend about Benjamin Disraeli, whose response to an anti-Semite was, "When your ancestors were living in caves, mine were writing the Talmud." A droll modern variant is, "When your ancestors were living in caves, mine already had diabetes."

---

1. Danish coin

The Anglo-Jewish writer Israel Zangwill was once at a dinner party next to a British matron. Bored with the conversation, he inadvertently let out a large yawn.
The matron turned to him and said, "Sir, I fear being swallowed up in that large Jewish mouth."
"Madam, you have no cause for concern," replied Zangwill. "My religion prohibits it."

Moses Montefiore, the wealthy Jewish philanthropist, was once at a dinner where a guest was holding forth on his recent trip to Japan. When asked what he found noteworthy, the traveler replied, "I was most pleased with the fact that Japan has neither pigs nor Jews."
Montefiore replied, "Perhaps we can travel together next time and rectify the situation."

A variant of this properly belongs in the Heretics, Atheists, Freethinkers, Converts category.

An atheist decides to bait his rabbi. "Rabbi, our tradition says, if one sees a mad dog, one should sit quietly. But, if one sees a rabbi, one should stand. So what does one do if one sees both a mad dog and a rabbi?"
The rabbi replies, "I really don't know. Why don't you and I walk down the street and see what happens?"

NAZIS

Amazing as it may seem, there's a considerable trove of Jewish jokes about Hitler and the Nazis:

> Hitler's finance minister is trying to convince him that throwing all the Jews out of business will hurt the German economy.
> "Mein Führer, they are very good businessmen, better than the average German. We need them."
> "Nonsense!" shouts Hitler. "Our Aryans are just as good, if not better!"
> "Let me show you what I mean," says the minister.
> They disguise themselves and enter a German shop.
> "We'd like to purchase a left-handed tea service," says the Minister.
> "Sorry," says the Aryan owner, "never heard of such a thing."
> They leave and go to a Jewish shop. "We'd like to purchase a left-handed tea service," says the minister. The owner goes into the back and returns a few minutes later, carrying a tea service with all the cup handles turned to the left.
> "This is the very last one in all of the Reich," says the Jew. "I'm afraid it's quite expensive."
> The minister pays the asking price, and he and Hitler leave with the service.
> "See what I mean?" says the minister.
> "Just luck," says the Führer, "the Jew had the last left-handed tea service in Germany!"

A German Jew loses his livelihood after the imposition of the Nuremberg Laws. He looks for some way to eke out a living. One day, he sees a notice that a circus is hiring performers. What does he know about circuses? Nothing. But a job's a job. He presents himself at the circus.
The manager tells him, "The job we are offering is a little unusual. We've lost our old lion. We need someone to dress up in a lion suit, do the tricks, and pretend to be ferocious."
The Jew readily agrees. How hard could it be? So he dresses up in the suit and waits for his cue. When the time comes, he runs around the cage in the

center ring, roars at the lion tamer, and jumps up and down on the various stands.

All goes brilliantly until the ramp to the cage is opened and in rushes a tiger. It roars, it froths, it bares its teeth, it tries to attack the "lion." The Jew is terrified. Sure his life is coming to an end, he begins to recite the Credo, "Shma yisroel, adonoy eloheynu, adonoy ekhod."[1]

To which, the tiger replies, "Barukh shem kvod malkhuso leyolam voed."[2] The second half!

"What?" says the Jew. "You're not a real tiger?"

"What do you think?" replies the tiger. "You're the only Jew working in Germany?"

Note the "double climax" typical of many Jewish jokes. The joke could simply have ended with the "tiger" reciting the prayer.

It's just after Kristallnacht. Adolph Levy comes to a German court and requests a change of name. The German judge glares down at him.

"No more will you Jews be able to camouflage yourselves as Aryans! Levy is your name, and Levy it will remain!"

"Fine with me," says Levy. "It's the Adolph I want to change—to Yisroel."

A German teacher asks Lotte Fein, the one remaining Jewish student in her high school class, "Who is the cause of all our woes?"

Lotte replies, "The Jews. And the bicyclists."

"Why the bicyclists?" asks the teacher.

"Why the Jews?"

At the end of World War II, some Jews liberated from the concentration camps were offered the opportunity to immigrate. Some opted for America. Others opted for France or England. One Jew asks for immigration papers to Australia.

"But it's so far," says the immigration official.

The Jew fixes him with a cold stare. "From what?"

---

1. See Glossary, under "Shma."
2. See Glossary, under "Shma."

Here's one from America:

> Two Jews are sitting on the New York City subway in 1942. One is reading the Yiddish *Forverts*; the other is reading the Nazi *Shtürmer*.
> The first one asks, "Why are you reading that anti-Semitic paper?"
> "It makes me feel good," he replies.
> "What are you talking about?" asks the stunned *Forverts* reader.
> "Simple. What do you read in your paper? The Jews are being ruined economically, persecuted, starved, and deported. What do I read? The Jews are all rich. We own the banks. We control the governments of the world …"

THE SOVIET UNION

The Soviet Union and its satellites tried maintaining the pretense they had abolished anti-Semitism. A wholly different type of humor grew up around that pretense.

> Vladimir goes for a job at a large Moscow firm. The head of personnel asks if there is anything in Vladimir's past they should know.
> "Yes," says Vladimir, "my grandfather was a general in the army of the last czar."
> "Please, comrade," replies the personnel chief, "we are not barbarians. That was more than a half-century ago. We do not hold grudges. Anything else?"
> "In fact, yes," says Vladimir, "my great-grandmother was a Jew."
> "Comrade," replies the head of personnel, "this is the Soviet Union. We are not prejudiced against any religion. But, come to think of it, your grandfather's service in the czar's army may present a problem."

A rumor is heard there will be fresh meat at a Moscow butcher shop. By 6:00 AM, the line stretches around the block. No delivery is yet in sight. By 9:00 AM, still no delivery. The official in charge announces, "There won't be enough meat for all of you. Jews, get out of line, and go home."
The Jews leave. At noon, the official announces to the line, "I've just received word that the delivery has been canceled. You can all go home."
One Russian turns to the other and says, "Those damn Jews. They get all the breaks."

Abramovich begins worrying, with all the firings of Jews, he will lose his job at the Soviet scientific institute. So, to play it safe, he converts.
A week later, a list of the institute workers fired appears. All Jews and Abramovich. He marches into the office of the head of the institute and asks, "Why did you fire me? I'm not a Jew."
"Yes, I know," says the head. "We had to include you so that no one could claim we're anti-Semitic."

A reporter is interviewing a Russian Jewish immigrant to Israel.

"So how was it with your economic status in Russia?"
"I couldn't complain," replies the immigrant.
"What about political rights?" asks the reporter.
"Couldn't complain."
"Religious prejudice?"
"Couldn't complain."
"So tell me, I don't understand, why have you immigrated to Israel?"
"Ah," says the immigrant, "Here I can complain!"

There is a nonpolitical American Jewish variant of this in which a Jew transfers from Swedish Covenant Hospital to Beth Israel Hospital. The point of this version is the difference in culture between Jews and Protestants.

"How was the food? The service? The care?"
"Couldn't complain."
"So why'd you transfer?"
"Here I can complain!"

A Jew is sitting on the street in Moscow reading a Hebrew primer. A Russian policeman begins hassling him. "Why are you learning Hebrew? Are you one of those Zionist traitors?"
"Not at all," says the Jew," but I understand, in heaven, they speak Hebrew." The policeman replies, "And suppose, when you die, you aren't going to heaven."
"Not a problem," says the Jew. "I already speak Russian."

Sofia, a Soviet Jewish artist, is ordered to paint a mural in the Kremlin. The theme: Lenin's period in Zurich, for which no painting exists. Sofia agrees and sets to work.
After three months, she announces she has completed the job. The Politburo gathers for the unveiling. The drape comes down, revealing a painting of a large bedroom with the Kremlin seen through the window. In the bed is Leon Trotsky, wearing only his glasses. Krupskaya, Mrs. Lenin, wears nothing.
"But where," demands the Politburo, "is Lenin?"
Sofia replies, "In Zurich."

Yuri, a Russian Jew, gets a knock on the door at 2:00 AM. "Who is it?" he asks.
"The mailman," comes the reply.
He opens the door. Three agents of the KGB confront him.

"We have heard a rumor you are trying to immigrate to Israel."

"It's true," says Yuri.

"Why, you Zionist traitor? What does Israel have that the Soviet motherland doesn't?"

"Well," says Yuri, "for one thing, the mailman only comes during the day."

POLAND

Polish Jews, subjected to both Polish and Communist anti-Semitism, have their own brand of humor. Here's one from the last century:

> A Jew is sitting across from a Pole on a train.
> The Pole says, "I can see from your Jewish nose that all you want is to defile our Christian maidens."
> The Jew doesn't reply. Some time passes.
> The Pole asks, "Hey, Jew, what time is it?"
> The Jew doesn't reply. The Pole asks again. Again no reply.
> Finally, the Pole shouts, "Hey Jew, are you deaf?"
> The Jew answers, "No, I hear you. But I figure, if you can tell so much about me from my nose, you ought to be able to guess the time just by knowing my watch is in my pocket."

> A Polish Jew in the 1960s inherits 20,000 zlotys. He asks his rabbi what to do with it.
> The rabbi replies, "Put it in the Polish National Bank."
> "But the bank could fail," says the Jew.
> "That's not very likely," says the rabbi. "It's backed by the Polish government."
> "But the government could collapse," worries the Jew.
> "That's also not likely," his rabbi reassures him. "Poland is backed by the might of the Soviet Union."
> "But the Soviet Union itself could fall," persists the Jew.
> The rabbi smiles. "Wouldn't that be worth 20,000 zlotys?"

When the Gomulka persecutions of 1968–1972 drove most of the remnant of Polish Jewry out, the story goes they were only allowed to change zlotys into two kilograms of silver at most. One poor "Yankl come lately" discovers most of the silver is already sold. He finds himself finally in an icon shop and spies a silver Christ on the cross.

"I'd like to buy that, but how much does it weigh?"
The storekeeper puts it on the scale and says, "Two-and-a-half kilograms."
Yankl asks, "How much without the acrobat?"

There's an American variant of this, which does not deal with anti-Semitism, but with the Jews' perennial doubt about the virgin birth.

> Goldstein, retired to Florida, finds himself bored, so he looks for a business to buy. He sees an ad: "Religious articles store for sale." He pays a visit and finds it's a Christian store. What the heck. Business is business. It'll keep him busy. Anyway, this is America. He buys the store.
> His biggest sale item is crosses—with Jesus, without Jesus—crosses. After a month, he's running low on stock. He checks the list of suppliers and finds South Florida Christian Items, Inc.
> He calls SFCI, Inc. and tells them, "This is Goldstein, the new owner of Dade County Religious Articles. I'm running low on crosses. Can you send me two gross?"
> To which, the voice at SFCI, Inc. replies, "With or without the mamzer?"[1]

---

1. Bastard

AMERICAN JEWISH HUMOR

American Jewish humor is generally quite different from its predecessors. To be sure, the Jews encountered anti-Semitism here, and they reacted to it with jokes. But the preponderance of this humor is more about assimilation, acculturation, encounter, dialogue, and friendly competition than about persecution. As Jews immigrated at the end of the nineteenth century to the United States (and other countries willing to extend them full civil rights), a new set of conditions arose to try them. Instead of constant oppression, they now had to deal with just how much they would assimilate into the surrounding culture, what they would gain, and what they might lose. These questions continue engaging us today. Like all such existential problems, they are a source of humor.

In this section, we find jokes by Jews about both Gentiles and Jews. The categories are more blurred than in the earlier sections. For example, do the many American Jewish jokes about priests, ministers, and rabbis belong here in Laughing Outward where I have put them, or, more properly, in the section above, Laughing Inward? Either or both. And that's what is so uniquely American. (In fact, I stuck a few American jokes in Laughing Inward. Remember "Where was Jesus born?" Not to mention the one just before this section.) Even indigenous "Laughing Inward" Jewish communal types, such as fund-raisers, are so quintessentially the products of the Jewish interaction with America that I have placed them here.

Anyway, I warned you in the introduction that categories are artificial constructs. So stop trying to make me feel guilty.

IMMIGRANTS

Berl, Merl, and Shmerl decide to immigrate to America from Poland. They land at Ellis Island, where they are advised to change their names to something more American.
Berl has been reading Yiddish translations of Westerns and promptly changes his name to Buck.
Merl, not to be outdone, changes his to Muck.
Shmerl goes back to Poland.

Rabinovich manages to acquire false papers to get out of Russia and onto a steamer to America. He studies and studies the papers to memorize his new name. As sometimes happens, he overstudies himself into a state of anxiety. He arrives at Ellis Island. The immigration officer asks his name.
He thinks for a minute and blurts out, "Definitely not Rabinovich!"

An immigrant Jew applies for a job in a wholesale clothing store on New York's Lower East Side.
"What's your name?" asks Mr. Schwartz, the owner, an earlier immigrant himself.
"Shawn Ferguson," replies the applicant.
"Are you joking?" asks Mr. Schwartz, "How did you get such a name?"
"Well," says the Jew, "my original name was Moishe Bernstein, but you yourself know what it was like getting out of Europe. So, I bought some papers with a different name. I tried and tried to memorize it, but I got so flustered that, when the Ellis Island immigration officer asked my name, I couldn't remember. So, I cried out in Yiddish, 'Shoyn fargesn!' (I forgot already!) And so I became Shawn Ferguson."

An elderly Jew immigrates to America in 1900. His daughter, already there some years, is explaining to him how to use the telephone.
"You see, Papa, with one hand, you hold the receiver. With the other, you dial the number."
Her father turns to her in puzzlement, "With what do I speak?"

PATRIOTS

It's the 1950s. A Hassidic Jew from Brooklyn travels to the South on business. He's walking down the main street of Tupelo, Mississippi, attracting a crowd of gawkers, who begin following him, pointing and laughing. He ignores the entourage as long as he can, but finally he's had enough. He turns around, puts his hands on his hips, and says "Vots de metter, you neveh seen a Yenkee?"

An English story deals with the same theme:

A Hassid lives with his son in a community north of London populated by their sect. One day, the young man decides to seek his fortune in the big city. He packs his suitcase and takes the train down to London.
He isn't there long before he realizes he'll have to get himself Anglicized if he wants to make it in business. So, off he goes to Saville Row, where he exchanges his Hassidic garb for a three-piece pin-striped suit, a homburg, and an umbrella. Then he goes off to the barber, where he has his beard and peyes shaved off.
The transformation indeed works. Within six months, he is well on his way to becoming a wealthy businessman. But he misses his father, so he calls and convinces the old man to join him in his fancy new digs. The father packs a suitcase and takes the train to Victoria Station, where he is met by his son, whom he scarcely recognizes.
"What happened to you, my boy?"
"Well, Papa," says the son, "in order to live here, one must become completely English."
"Me too?" asks the father.
"Yes, indeed," says the son.
"Okay," agrees the old man, "what do I have to do?"
So off they go to Saville Row, where he is outfitted in a three-piece suit, complete with homburg and umbrella.
"That's it? Now I'm English?"

"Not yet, Papa. Now we go to the barber." So off they go.

The old man sits down in the chair, and the barber shaves off his luxuriant white beard.

"Now I'm English?"

"Not quite yet, Papa."

Snip! Off comes one peye.

"Now I'm English?"

"Almost, Papa."

Snip! As the second peye falls, the old man bursts into tears.

"Papa," says the son, "what's the matter?"

The old man sobs, "We gave up India!"

Mrs. Yoshimura, a Japanese senior citizen on her first trip to America, comes into Macy's department store in Manhattan. She walks up to Mrs. Cohen, a Jewish saleslady about her own age, and says, "Excuse me, can you tell me where the cosmetics department is?"

"Oh," says Mrs. Cohen, "Pearl Harbor you could find?"

Just as Jews in the Old Country were proud of their respective towns, so are American Jews partisans of the cities in which they live. New York Jews carry it to extremes. Mrs. Goldberg and Mrs. Fein take their first trip to the West Coast. They get off the plane in Los Angeles in the middle of a heat wave.

"Boy, is it hot here!" says Mrs. Goldberg.

"What do you expect?" says Mrs. Fein. "We're 3,000 miles from the ocean."

EDUCATION

A Jewish boy from a secular family in the Bronx decides to get an apartment in Washington Heights in north Manhattan and enroll in Yeshivah University. Two months later, he returns to the Bronx for a visit. His father opens the door to see his son in a yarmulke and kapote and with a beard and peyes. The father calls in to his wife, "Sadie, come here, and take a look at Joe College!"

Another Jewish boy is a very bad student. He doesn't study and cuts up in class. His parents finally decide to enroll him in a private school, a Catholic school in fact, which they've heard is good with difficult students. So it turns out. The boy comes home with a B+ average and a commendation for good behavior.
"How come?" ask his happy, but bewildered, parents.
"How come?" says the boy. "Check out their chapel. Have you seen what they do to guys who misbehave?"

Here is a tale that can serve as revenge for all of us who experienced anti-Jewish quotas in college:

> A college president tells his dean of admissions they are getting too many Jews at the school and they need to start changing the balance.
> The president says, "Use the interviews with prospective freshmen to weed out the Jews. Don't ask overt questions. That's illegal. Find some clever ways to get the information."
> So the dean does this. He eliminates all the obvious ones: Cohen, Levy, Goldstein, and other Jewish or Jewish-sounding names. For the rest, he questions where they live, whether they're interested in religion, if they've ever been to Israel ...
> One day, he gets a candidate with the neutral name of Green. He is from a mixed neighborhood and has never been abroad. He questions the kid about his interests and if he is religious, but he comes up empty on all counts.

Finally, in desperation, he asks, "Mr. Green, do you happen to speak Yiddish?"
Green replies, "Enough to get around on this campus."

SPORTS

Sports is another topic that is characteristically American Jewish.

A Jewish gambler, newly arrived in America, gets himself a bookie and starts betting on basketball. The first day, he bets $100 on the New York Knicks against the Chicago Bulls. Loses. The next day, he bets $200 on the Seattle Supersonics against the Utah Jazz. Loses again. The third day, he bets $400 on the Minnesota Timberwolves against the New Jersey Nets. Loses again.

The fourth day he calls his bookie and asks for some more basketball action. "No games today," says the bookie. "How about hockey?"

"Hockey?" replies the immigrant. "What the heck do I know about hockey?"

A Jewish golfer is a real duffer. He's never done better than ten over par. One day, he's playing and sees a foursome of ultra-Orthodox Jews playing amazingly good golf. He watches for a while and finally goes over to ask them the secret of their skill.

"Religion," they reply. "Are you Jewish?"

He says yes.

"Okay, here's what you have to do. Pray three times a day. Keep kosher. And join the Orthodox shul."[1]

Our hero gets down his old talles and tefillin and prays regularly. He gets two new sets of dishes, makes his home strictly kosher, joins the Orthodox shul down the street. But his game does not improve.

Two months later, he encounters the same pious foursome, playing their usual under-par game.

"I don't know what I'm doing wrong," he complains. "I did everything you said."

"You pray regularly?" they ask.

"Three times a day."

"Keep kosher?"

"Strictly."

---

1. Synagogue

"Did you join an Orthodox shul?"
"Yes, I joined Anshe Sholem, just down the street."
"Ah," say the foursome. "That's the problem. Anshe Sholem's the tennis shul."

A rabbi sneaks off one Shabbes to the golf course. He tees off and hits a long drive. God produces a wind that lofts the ball several hundred yards, right into the first hole.
"But he's violating the Sabbath. Why are you rewarding his behavior?" asks the Angel Gabriel.
"Rewarding?" says God. "I'm punishing him. Who can he tell?"

Al Goldberg approaches his rabbi during the High Holy Days between Rosh Hashonah and Yom Kippur.
"Rabbi, I have a dilemma. The first game of the World Series is being played the same time as Kol Nidre."[2]
"Al," replies the rabbi, "isn't that what a VCR is for?"
Al's face lights up. "You mean I can tape Kol Nidre?"

Yeshiva University decided to field a rowing crew. Unfortunately, they lose contest after contest. They just can't figure out what's wrong. They decide to send out a spy to see how the other colleges do it.
So, they send Yankel to spy on the Harvard crew. Yankel heads off to Cambridge to keep a close watch on the Charles River. Some time later, he returns, bursting with enthusiasm.
"I have it. I know the secret of winning. They have eight guys rowing and only one guy shouting."

---

2. The main prayer of the Yom Kippur Eve service; used to connote the service itself

ALRIGHTNIKS AND SHOW-OFFS

Rich Jews and social climbers in America, like their European counterparts, come in for their share of ridicule. Here, the theme is likely to be parvenus, arrivistes, or, as Yinglish calls them, alrightniks.

> Maurice and Mollie have become so wealthy they decide to commission a famous artist to do a mural on a wall of their home. The artist is in there for three months, working in complete secrecy.
> Finally, he announces he is finished. Maurice and Mollie invite all their friends over for the unveiling. The artist sweeps the cloth aside, and they see a completely blank wall with a small red circle in the center.
> "Oooh! Aaah!" Their friends are very impressed with this avant-garde creation. Maurice and Mollie are so pleased they hire the artist on the spot to do another wall. This time, he's cloistered for a full half year.
> At the unveiling, their friends are gathered around. The artist sweeps aside the cloth, and they see a completely blank wall with a small red circle in the center and, circumscribed around the circle, a yellow triangle. Mollie turns to Maurice and says, "Don't you think it's a little busy?"

> S. Merrill Blackwood (né Shmerl Schwartzwald) tries joining the posh, restricted Long Island Hills Country Club. He does fine on the application form, happily falsifying his origins, until he hits the line for religion and writes, "I am of the goyish[1] persuasion."

> Four women find themselves sharing a table at a posh Soho[2] singles bar. They introduce themselves.
> "My name is Crane," says the first.
> "Kane," says the second.
> The third introduces herself as "Chaney."
> The fourth smiles and says, "Also Cohen."

---

1. Gentile
2. New York City area; short for "South of Houston Street"; very yuppified. (As we say in Yinglish, "Fency shmency.")

A NEW TYPE, MADE IN USA

Just as general Jewish humor deals with indigenous characters such as rabbis, circumcisers, and shnorrers, American Jewry has its own unique creation.

> A circus strongman takes a lemon and squeezes it as hard as he can until its juice runs out.
> "Anyone who can get another drop out of this lemon wins fifty dollars," he challenges his audience.
> One bodybuilder after another tries … and fails.
> Finally, a little, neatly dressed fellow in the front row says, "Let me give it a shot."
> The audience snickers as he mounts the stage and takes the lemon in his small hand. He squeezes, and a spurt of juice sprays the onlookers.
> "That's amazing," marvels the strongman. "What do you do for a living?"
> The little fellow answers, "I'm a fund-raiser for the UJA."[1]

> Sam and Bessie decide to celebrate retirement by taking a cruise to the South Pacific. As luck would have it, a typhoon disables the ship. The passengers and crew manage to wash up on an island. Unfortunately, the captain announces the island is nowhere to be found on any maps and the radio was lost in the shipwreck.
> "I'm afraid our chances of rescue are very slim. We may be marooned here for the rest of our lives."
> Sam turns to Bessie. "Did we pay our annual UJA pledge?"
> "Not yet."
> Sam smiles. "They'll find us."

---

1. United Jewish Appeal

DIALOGUE I: JEWS AND GENTILES

Typical of American Jewish humor is "friendly dialogue" between Jews and Gentiles. In these jokes, the cultures don't actually clash. They just kind of bump up against each other.

> Two friends, Sol and Frank, of Jewish and Italian origin, respectively, are trying to decide where to vacation.
> "How about the Poconos?" proposes Frank. "A lot of my people go there."
> "Nah," says Sol, "let's go to the Catskills. A great place to meet the ladies."
> Frank is hesitant. "Sure, I'd like to meet some nice ladies, but they're Jewish. What happens if they ask me about myself?"
> Sol has his advice ready. "You tell them your name is Frank. You're from the Bronx. You're a manufacturer. If they ask what you manufacture, you tell them talleysim.[1] Can you remember that? Talleysim."
> "What's it mean?" asks Frank.
> "Never mind," Sol reassures him. "Once you say 'talleysim,' they won't even question your origins."
> And so it goes. The first night in the Catskills, Sol and Frank are at the resort bar. A very attractive woman strikes up a conversation with Frank.
> "What's your name?"
> "Frank."
> "Where are you from?"
> "The Bronx."
> "What do you do?"
> "I'm a manufacturer."
> "What do you manufacture?"
> "Talleysim," says Frank without hesitation.

---

1. Plural of *talles*, prayer shawl. The shawl contains a band with Hebrew writing at the collar and a series of elaborately knotted fringes at the ends.

The woman thinks for a few seconds and says, "You know, I've always wondered what those Hebrew words around the collar say."
Frank replies, "I wouldn't know. We just make the sleeves."

Sol himself had an unfortunate experience with his own talles. He was used to taking it to a Jewish dry cleaner every month or so. One day, he brings it in and notices a Korean now owns the establishment.
Sol leaves the talles and comes back the next week to pick it up. The Korean hands him the bill of twenty-five dollars.
A shocked Sol remonstrates, "This used to cost only five dollars!"
The Korean replies, "You know how long it took me to get all the knots out?"

Mr. Levine decides to sell his condo. The first person to answer the classified ad is Mr. Shanahan. Levine opens the door to him, remembering to touch the mezuzah[2] attached thereto. He takes Shanahan through the apartment. On each door is a mezuzah. Levine touches each one as he enters the room.
At the conclusion of the tour, Shanahan says, "I love this place, and I'm glad to pay your asking price. But only on condition you leave the security system."

Meyer and Rachel, a young Orthodox Jewish married couple, are expecting their first baby. Unfortunately, Esther's water breaks on the Sabbath when Jews aren't supposed to work or drive, but they have no choice but to call for a taxi to take them to the hospital.
Because they want to try to minimize the Sabbath violation, they ask the dispatcher to send a non-Jewish driver.
The taxi arrives. As Meyer and Rachel get in, they overhear the radio dispatcher ask the driver, "Have you picked up the anti-Semites yet?"

---

2. A parchment with part of Deuteronomy (the fifth book of the Bible) enclosed in a small case, attached to the doorposts of Jewish homes. Religious Jews touch it whenever they pass through a doorway.

DIALOGUE II: PRIESTS, MINISTERS, AND RABBIS

One form of uniquely American Jewish humor is the rabbi/priest/minister joke. The theme is friendly rivalry, virtually inconceivable in earlier periods and other countries.

> A Catholic church adjoins a synagogue. Each congregation wants to show how well it treats its clergyman. The Catholics take up a collection and buy their priest a Mercedes. The Jews buy their rabbi a Jaguar. The priest goes out to his Mercedes and sprinkles it with holy water. The rabbi goes out to his Jaguar and saws two inches off the tailpipe.
>
> A priest and a rabbi have been friends for many years.
> One day, the priest asks the rabbi, "Tell me the truth. Have you ever had ham?"
> "Well," replies the rabbi, "because you're such a good friend, I'll confess to you. Before I was ordained, I tried ham once. But let me ask you something. Have you ever had sex?"
> "Well," replies the priest, "because we're such good friends, I'll tell you. Before I took holy orders, I tried sex once."
> "Better than ham, wasn't it?" says the rabbi.
>
> A priest, a minister, and a rabbi, friends for many years, are talking.
> "I have to confess to you, my good friends," says the priest, "something I've never told anyone. I can't control my need for alcohol. After each service, I drink an entire bottle of sacramental wine."
> "And I," says the minister, "must also tell you my darkest secret. I cannot control my lust. I've had affairs with countless female congregants."
> The rabbi says nothing.
> "What about you?" ask his colleagues. "Don't you have any fault you're willing to share with us? It's only fair after we've unburdened ourselves to you."

"Well," says the rabbi, "I have one, but I'm afraid it will upset you too much if I tell you."

"Come now," his friends urge him," we're men of the cloth. Nothing can shock us."

"Okay," says the rabbi, "For the life of me, I can't keep a secret."

A priest and a rabbi are good friends. One day, the priest invites the rabbi to listen as he hears confession.

The first penitent says, "Father, I have sinned. I committed adultery three times this week."

"Say ten Hail Marys, and put five dollars in the poor box," says the priest.

A second penitent also confesses, "Father, I have sinned. I committed adultery three times this week."

"Say ten Hail Marys, and put five dollars in the poor box," is again the priest's reply.

The priest suddenly gets an urgent call.

"Can you take over for a minute?" he begs the rabbi. "They'll never know the difference."

The rabbi reluctantly agrees and takes his place in the confessional. In comes a penitent, who says, "Father, I have sinned. I committed adultery twice this week."

"Go out, and do it once more," says the rabbi. "They're on special. Three for five dollars."

A priest, a minister, and a rabbi all serve congregations in a town near the Canadian border. They are good friends. Even more, they are drinking buddies. One day, several sheets to the wind, they decide to make a bet. Who can convert a bear? So they all stagger into the North Woods.

Three days later, the priest and minister visit the rabbi in the hospital.

Swathed in bandages, the rabbi asks, "How did it go?"

"Well," says the priest, "I went into the woods with a vial of holy water. Suddenly a bear rushed at me. Just as he was about to grab me, I threw the holy water at him and cried, 'I hereby baptize you in the name of the Father, the Son, and the Holy Ghost.' The bear dropped to its knees and clasped its hands together. I left."

The minister says, "I went into the woods and stayed near the river. A bear came rushing at me, so I ran down to the river and jumped in. He followed me. As soon as he was in the water, I shouted, 'You are now baptized and are born again!' The bear became as gentle as a lamb and began emitting soft growls as if he was praying. I left."

"But what happened to you?" they ask.

"You ever try to circumcise a bear?"

GENTILES: SUCH PUZZLING FOLK

Jews often find themselves puzzled at Christian belief and practice. We suspect, for example, the secret of Christianity's popularity is the promise of an afterlife and the bacon cheeseburger.

The bemusement of the Jews also reaches to other aspects of Christianity.

> A group of Hassidim, seeking shelter from a sudden rainstorm, run into a Catholic church right in the middle of the service when newly minted nuns take their marriage vows to Christ.
>
> The Jews try remaining quiet and unobtrusive, but they are, of course, noticed. The Mother Superior comes over and asks, "What are you doing here at the marriage ceremony between these girls and our Lord?"
>
> The Hassidim reply, "We're from the groom's side."

Christian Scientists come in for their share of ribbing:

> A concert is about to begin to a packed audience at Carnegie Hall when a voice with a Yiddish accent is suddenly heard crying out, "Is there a Christian Scientist in the house? Is there a Christian Scientist in the house?"
>
> Finally, a woman comes down to the elderly Jew and says, "I'm a Christian Scientist."
>
> "Oh, good," says the Jew. "Would you mind changing seats? I'm sitting in a draft."

> A poor Jew rents an attic room from a Christian Scientist landlord. The Jew is sick for several weeks with a flu and fever and cannot pay the rent. The landlord comes down and berates his tenant for malfeasance.
>
> "Sickness is entirely in your head. Just talk yourself into believing you're healthy, and you will be."
>
> The Jew replies, "Why don't you just talk yourself into believing the rent is paid?"

POPERY

Another peculiarly American Jewish set of jokes has to do with Jews and the Pope. Certainly, some Jews have met the Pope, but not as many as like to claim that honor. Why? Who knows?

Morrie takes a two-week vacation from the Garment Center and visits Italy. He comes back, and his friends ask him, "So, did you meet the Pope?"
"Sure," says Morrie.
"So how would you describe him?"
"A 38 long."

Nathan and Shirley Altman come back from a trip to Italy.
"So," ask their friends, "did you meet the Pope?"
"Of course!"
"So what did you think?"
Shirley sniffs. "He was okay. Her I didn't care for."

Goldstein brags he knows everyone. His friend Shulweiss finally decides to call his bluff. "Do you know the Pope?"
"What a question! Of course I know the Pope. We're good buddies," says Goldstein.
"Okay," says Shulweiss, "here's two tickets to Rome. You and I are going, and I want to see you with the Pope."
So off they go. Twenty-four hours later, they're in the square outside St. Peter's. The Pope is scheduled to bless the crowd in fifteen minutes.
"So, big shot?" says Shulweiss.
"So, watch," says Goldstein and disappears into the crowd.
Fifteen minutes later, a roar goes up, and Shulweiss sees the Pope appear on the balcony—with Goldstein at his side! Shulweiss is dumbfounded.
As he stands there with his mouth open, a little Italian fellow taps him on the shoulder and says, "Hey, who's the guy up there with Goldstein?"

Sadie Siegel returns from a trip to Italy.
"So, what'd you think of the Vatican?" her friends ask.

"Nice," she replies, "if you like modern."

I'd like to think the deeper meaning of that joke is the relatively late arrival of Christianity vis-à-vis Judaism. But probably not.

Part Three
Language Humor, Mainly Yiddish

Jewish migrations, involuntary and voluntary, have led to one form of humor that I think is unique, in degree, if not in kind. That is the humor of language. The specific difficulty of maintaining language for two millennia without a country of our own has led to a focus on—even an obsession with—the spoken and written word. The appellation "People of the Book" connotes a great deal more than simply adherents of the Bible. The nearly universal literacy throughout history of Jewish males and the comparatively high literacy of females as well speaks to an unusual attachment to languages. These include our own: Hebrew, Yiddish, Ladino/Judesmo, Judaeo-Arab (Moghrabi), and others, as well as the languages of our various countries of residence. This obsession with language brings a rich trove of humor with it.

In this section, I'll deal with Yiddish-related humor. Within such humor, we find several subgroups:

- Jokes in Yiddish, based on the idiosyncrasies of the language[1]

- Language contact jokes, in which the Yiddish-speaking Jew encounters other tongues with comical results

---

1. Don't worry. I'll translate.

- Bilingual and multilingual jokes. These include the ones in which the entire setup is in English, the punch line is in Yiddish, and only the cognoscenti get it.
- Jokes that can be translated from Yiddish to English with varying degrees of success.

Before we start, here's a beaut that summarizes the Jewish view on language:

A cat is sitting by a mouse hole. She opens her mouth and says, "Squeak."
A mouse sticks its head out of the hole. Snap! The cat grabs and eats it.
She turns to her kitten and says, "You see how important it is to speak a foreign language?"

PURE YIDDISH JOKES

These jokes are originally in Yiddish. I will tell them here in English with the Yiddish punch line immediately translated in a footnote. (These are not to be confused with those in Group Three for which the setup must be in English.)

There are various types of pure Yiddish humor. One is based on the double entendre.

The word *sheyn* in Yiddish literally means "pretty" or "handsome," but it also connotes spiritual beauty.

> A Jew comes to a strange town looking for his old friend.
> He stops another Jew on the street and asks him, "Do you know Reb Yankl, the shoemaker?"
> "Reb Yankl ..." muses the other Jew. "You mean Reb Yankl with the drooping eyelid?"
> "Yes."
> "And the crooked nose with the wart on the end?"
> "Yes."
> "And the three missing teeth in the front?"
> "Yes, yes."
> "And the pockmarked skin?"
> "Yes, that's him exactly!"
> "Oh, yes, I know him. A sheyner yid!"[1]

Grob also has two meanings in Yiddish. It can refer to either a deep voice or a coarse manner. The following story depends on this double entendre. It is also the one of this entire collection that only works when told aloud. But here goes:

---

1. A beautiful Jew

During the service, a cantor announces he is looking for someone who can sing bass in the choir. After the service, there comes a knock on the cantor's office door. A small, rotund Jew walks in.
"Can I help you?" asks the cantor.
In a very high-pitched voice, the Jew replies, "You're looking for a bass?"
"Yes. Do you know anyone who sings bass?"
"I'm a bass!" replies the high-pitched Jew.
"Kent ir redn a bisl grober?"[2] asks the cantor.
"Yeh," answers the Jew, still in soprano range. "Ikh hob dir in drerd!"[3]

Hobn in drerd literally means "to have in the ground." "Go to Hell" is one reasonable translation; another connotation is not giving a fig about anyone.

A Jew sees an old friend eating in a restaurant. He sits down at the friend's table and asks, "So how's your wife?"
"Dead."
"Oh, I didn't know. I'm so sorry. And your father?"
"Dead."
"Also? How awful for you. What about your younger sister?"
"Dead."
"Good grief, what a catastrophe! How can it be that all of your loved ones have died?"
The Jew puts his fork down and says, "Ven ikh es, hob ikh alemen in drerd!"[4]

A second form of pure Yiddish humor finds its source in "fancy language," the juxtaposition of elegant linguistic constructions with situations bordering on the mundane, even the crude.

A long-married couple is asked the secret of their success.
The husband answers, "We agree on all issues except the agrarian question."
"The agrarian question?"
"Yeh, zi zogt, ikh zol lign in drerd, un ikh zog, zi zol lign in drerd!"[5]

---

2. Can you speak a bit deeper?
3. You can go to hell.
4. When I eat, I have everyone in the ground. (I don't give a fig for anybody.)
5. She says, I should lie in the ground (drop dead), and I say she should lie in the ground.

Like many languages, Yiddish has a formal and informal form of "you," as an object, aykh and dir, respectively.

> A boy comes home from kheder with a red ear.
> "What happened?" asks his father.
> "The melamed smacked me on the ear."
> "Why?"
> "Because I said to him, 'Ikh hob dir in drerd.'"
> The father smacks his other ear. "You hooligan! To a melamed you don't say, 'Ikh hob dir in drerd.' Have respect! To a melamed, you say, 'Ikh hob aykh in drerd!'"

There are several words for "die" in Yiddish. The fanciest is *nifter*, from the Hebrew root meaning to be freed, to shuffle off this mortal coil. It's a word simple Jews might not know. But they'd never admit it.

> Two friends meet on the street.
> "How's your wife?" asks the one.
> "Nifter," the other replies.
> "Ah, nifter shmifter, abi gezint!"[6]

There's an English version, "Cancer shmancer, as long as she has her health." Nice try, but it just doesn't make it. An uneducated Jew might not know *nifter*, the fancy word for "dead," but everyone knows cancer is a disease.

---

6. As long as she's healthy.

LANGUAGE CONTACT JOKES

Yiddish celebrated its one-thousandth birthday a few years ago. That makes it at least 200 years older than English. Yiddish and English have one important feature in common. They are what linguists call fusion languages. That is, they have several recognizable root languages, unlike, for example, Spanish or Italian, which primarily have Latin as their single source. Of course, many languages have elements of other sources. Spanish has some Arabic from the Moorish conquest, for example. But Yiddish and English have major contributions from several other, earlier tongues.

In the case of English, the sources are Germanic, primarily Anglo-Saxon and Norse as well as Norman French, which came over with William the Conqueror in 1066.

For Yiddish, the primary root languages are Hebrew; Judaeo-Aramaic; an old form of German; and East European Yiddish, a Slavic language. (There's also a smaller percentage of older Romance languages as well as Latin and Greek.)

In the modern period, Yiddish, with its older Germanic and Hebrew-Aramaic roots, has encountered modern German and modern Hebrew as well as English—in some cases with hilarious results.

Oddly enough, there is little humor around the Slavic component. At least I don't know any, except for a personal story the actor Morris Carnovsky told about taking a German course in which he succeeded by tarting up Yiddish words to sound more German. Unfortunately, when asked for the word for "duck" in German (Ente), he came up with *katzke*, from the Slavic-rooted Yiddish *katchke!*

Yiddish and German

The encounter with modern German provides a classic example of the Jewish penchant for turning adversity into laughter. Because Yiddish and German have about a fifty percent overlap in vocabulary, both pure German speakers and many Enlightenment Jews characterized Yiddish as a nonlanguage, a mere dialect, a jargon, or a "bastardized German." (No one ever called Norwegian a bastardized Danish or Italian a bastardized Spanish.)

Jews turned this on its head with a series of jokes in which the Yiddish-speaking Jew has pretensions he or she is actually speaking German. Inevitably, the Hebrew-Aramaic component sneaks in. The shortest example is the two-line dialogue:

"Sprechen Sie Deutsch?"[1]
"A shayle!"[2]

Shayle is pure Hebrew-rooted Yiddish.

Another one of this genre—and I think the greatest example of all—involves a discussion between a Russian and a Jew, in what the latter thinks is German. (Warning! This joke is loaded with Hebrew-Aramaic.)

> During a synagogue service in Czarist Russia, a young Jew suddenly stands up and begins shouting and cursing at the rabbi. The congregation is unable to calm the young man down and finally resorts to the virtually unheard-of. They have him arrested by the Russian police.
> After a few days, cooler heads prevail, and the community realizes it doesn't want one of its own, addled as he may be, sitting in a Russian jail. A delegation approaches the Russian police chief and asks for the boy's release. The chief is ready to do this, but he points out the aggrieved party, the rabbi himself, must come in to drop the charges. The rabbi is ready to do so, but he speaks no Russian. How will he explain?
> The police chief says, "I speak German. Does the rabbi?"
> Such a question! What Jew doesn't speak German?
> The police chief asks the rabbi, "Wollen Sie den Jungen Mann verzeihen?"[3]
> The rabbi replies, "Lekhaskhileh bin ikh of em geven moleh kas, aza sheygetz, mikh shelten in beys medresh, bshas kriyes toyreh, bifney kol am v'eydeh. Ober sof-kol-sof, meyleh, der bokher zitst in tfise shoyn lang genug, iz itzter bin ikh im moykhl mkhileh gemureh."[4]

---

1. Do you speak German? (German)
2. Such a question!
3. Will you forgive the young man? (German)
4. At first, I was full of fury, that scoundrel, cursing me in synagogue during the reading of the Torah, in front of the whole congregation. But finally, never mind, the lad has sat in jail long enough, so now I completely forgive him.

> Because about every other word of this German is Hebrew-Aramaic, the police chief cries, "Das ist kein Deutsch!"⁵
>
> The rabbi turns to his followers and mutters, "Ze ver lernt mir daytsh!"⁶

This joke contains several elements characteristic of Jewish humor in the old country. First, of course, the pretension that Yiddish is German. Second, the rabbi's pretension the Gentile is the ignorant one. Third, the double climax characteristic of much of Jewish humor. The tale is funny enough when the rabbi concludes his long explanation. However, his final comment gives the story an extra punch.

Because there is considerable overlap between Yiddish and German, it was often possible for the speaker of one to understand the other. Such an outcome was often undesirable from the Jews' point of view, and they developed a kind of code language in which they inserted a Hebrew equivalent of a German root word, even though it was the latter, not the former, which was correct Yiddish. A Gentile German speaker might easily understand one Jew saying "Her, der goy farshteyt"⁷ to another, but not "Zay shoymeah, der orel faromedt." It means the same thing, but it's in Hebrew-Yiddish code. Jewish criminals utilized this linguistic trick in much of their dealings, so much so that ordinary Jews thought of it as the province of the underworld.

> The tale is told of a German, a suspected horse thief, captured on the street by the Russian police.
>
> They are unable to question him, so they ask if anyone in the assembled crowd of onlookers can speak German. Naturally, a Jew presents himself as a translator. The police tell him to ask the German if he took the horse in question.
>
> The Jew, in best underworld Yiddish, asks, "Hostu gelakkhent dem sus?"⁸
>
> Because *gelakkhent* and *sus* are from Hebrew, the German replies (in perfect German) "Ich verstehe nicht."⁹
>
> The Jew turns to the police and says, "Not only is he a thief, he's a liar. He's not German!"

---

5. That's not German! (German)
6. Look who's teaching me German! (Yiddish)
7. Listen, the Gentile understands.
8. Did you take the horse?
9. I don't understand.

Related languages often have what the French call faux amis (false friends), that is, the same word has acquired different meanings. One such is schmecken, which, in German, means "to taste, to have flavor." In most Yiddish dialects, it means "to smell, to have an odor."

> A Jew orders a bowl of soup in a German restaurant. The waiter brings it. The Jew begins eating, and the solicitous waiter asks, "Das schmeckt?"[10]
> "Neyn, es shmekt nisht,"[11] replies the Jew.
> The waiter summarily removes the uneaten soup and returns with another bowl.
> The same scene is played out again ... and yet again. By the fourth bowl, the Jew hunches protectively over the bowl.
> When the waiter asks, "Das schmeckt?" the Jew replies angrily, "Yo, es shmekt! Es shtinkt! Nu loz mikh esn!"[12]

Yiddish and Hebrew

The encounter of modern Hebrew and Yiddish reflects in large measure the encounter of European Jews with modern Zionism and Israel. As with the Yiddish-German encounter, much of the humor has to do with linguistic pretensions.

> An American Jew, originally from Poland, visits Israel for the first time. He gets in a cab in Tel Aviv and addresses the driver as *balagole*. Indeed, it is a Hebrew-Yiddish word meaning driver, but it refers to a wagon driver in the old country. The Israeli driver corrects him with the modern Hebrew word.
> "I am not a *balagole*. I am a *nahag*."
> The Jew persists in calling the *nahag* a *balagole* and refuses to be corrected. The driver becomes increasingly angry.
> Finally, the Jew stubbornly asks, "So what's the difference anyway?"
> To which, the driver replies, "The difference is, with a *balagole*, the horse's ass is in the front!"

Little love has been lost between East European Ostjuden and German Jewish Yeckes. The former found the latter pretentious, while the latter considered the former unschooled and vulgar. (I am using the past tense here with some trepidation.)

---

10. Does it have flavor?
11. No, it doesn't smell.
12. Yes, it smells! It stinks! Now let me eat!

German Jewish immigrants often moved to Haifa, where it is claimed they spoke German to each other and Hebrew to their dogs.

> The story is told of such a German Jew who falls into Haifa Bay. Standing on the shore is an East European Jew, a Galitsianer, if you wish.
> The Yecke shouts "Hotziloni!"[13] to the Galitsianer.
> The Galitsianer shouts back, "Instead of such fancy Hebrew, better you should have learned to swim!"

There is a Chelm variant, in which a Jew is drowning and the onshore Chelmite yells, "Get back here, and learn to swim!"

The founders of modern Israel, most of them native Yiddish speakers, made Herculean efforts to master modern Hebrew as part of the ideology of transforming the Diaspora Jew. But sometimes the effort proved too much.

> On a broiling summer day in the 1950s, a busload of American Jewish tourists pulls up to Sde Boker, Ben Gurion's kibbutz, where they come upon the prime minister himself, discussing politics with President Yitskhak Ben Zvi in Yiddish.
> One tourist, ardent Zionist she, approaches and asks in Hebrew, "Lama atem lo midabrim ivrit?"[14]
> Ben Gurion turns to Ben Zvi and mutters, in Yiddish, "Fertzik grad, un zi vil az mir zoln redn hebreyish?"[15]

Yiddish and English

The encounter with English is of a rather different order. This tongue, representing a new life in a new country, is notoriously difficult with more exceptions than rules as well as the usual range of idiomatic expressions completely opaque to the novice. The immigrants eventually mastered their new language ... not, however, without some amusing results.

(As a warm-up exercise for this section, say the following words aloud: foible, spatula, ladle, svelte, lentil, garnished, varnished, bundle, satchel, mantle, girdle,

---

13. Literally "Save me," but a very flowery way of saying it.
14. Why aren't you speaking Hebrew?
15. 40°C (104°F), and she wants us to speak Hebrew?

goiter, squelch, box kite, farfetched, and landslide. Don't they sound like they should be Yiddish?)

"My wife's having an affair."
"Oh? Who's the caterer?"

"You've been sleeping with my wife!"
"I swear, not a wink!"

"A fly was sitting on my nose half the night."
"Why didn't you just brush it off?"
"I didn't realize it was dusty."

"That tiger belongs to the feline family."
"And they just went away and left it in a cage?"

An elderly Jewish lady is accosted on the street by a shabbily dressed man who says, "I haven't eaten anything in three days!"
"Force yourself."

An elderly Jewish man is run over. He's lying in the street when the paramedics arrive. As they load him carefully onto the stretcher, one asks, "Are you comfortable?"
He replies, "Thank God, I make a living."

An elderly Jewish lady is run over. A lawyer rushes to her side, hands her his card, and says, "Call me. I can get you damages."
The lady replies, "Damages I already have. What I need is repairs!"

Lithuanian Jews, or Litvaks, tend to transmute the Yiddish sh sound into a pure s. Other Jews refer to their dialect as Sabbesdik losn, a play on Shabbesdik loshn.[16] One such Litvak has the bad fortune to immigrate to the United States just as it enters World War I. No sooner has he become a citizen, than he is drafted and sent to basic training.

As the platoon is training in riflery, the Litvak stands uncomprehending during the commands of "Ready, aim, fire!" As soon as he hears "Cease fire," he begins blasting away. He is quickly overpowered by his fellow soldiers, who

---

16. Sabbath tongue

demand to know why he didn't heed the order to cease. He replies in injured tones, "Ikh hob gehert 'sis,' hob ikh gesosn!"[17]

It is a common Jewish superstition to never give a person's age without adding, "biz hundert tsvantsik" (to 120). If you don't wish them such a long life, the Angel of Death may hear their age and decide to cut their life short.

> In a New York City court, a Jewish immigrant is asked his age.
> The Yiddish interpreter, a young fellow, linguistically capable but unschooled in tradition, asks "Vi alt zayt ir?"[18]
> The elderly Jew replies, "Zibetsik, biz hundert tsvantsik."
> The confused interpreter tells the judge, "He says he's seventy to 120."
> "Tell him to narrow it down," says the judge.
> The interpreter tries again—with the same confusing results. The trial grinds to a halt. Finally, an elderly Jewish backbencher approaches the bailiff and asks if he can try. Why not?
> He turns to the witness and asks, "Vi alt zayt ir, biz hundert tsvantsik?"[19]
> To which, the witness happily replies, "Zibetsik!"

> A Jew is leaving Poland for America. His friend asks him if he knows any English.
> "Oui," he replies.
> "But that's French," says the friend.
> "Oh, I didn't know I also speak French!"

> Moishe Feigenbaum, newly arrived from Czarist Russia, is riding the New York City subway for the first time. He sees a Catholic priest across from him. Not recognizing the clerical garb (Russian Orthodox priests wear a quite different outfit), Moishe approaches him and says, "Mister, you got your shoyt on beckvards."
> "I'm a Father," replies the priest.
> "Fadder shmadder," says Moishe. "You still got your shoyt on beckvards."
> "You don't understand," says the priest. "I am a Father to thousands."
> "Mister," says Moishe, "never mind de shoyt. Better you should put your pents on beckvards!"

---

17. I heard *shoot*, so I shot. Or, as the Litvak might say, "I heard *soot*, so I sot. *Shoot* in other Yiddish dialects is *shis*. *Shot* is *geshosn*. Only a Litvak could make such a mistake. (Isn't it awful when you have to explain a joke?)
18. How old are you?
19. How old are you, to one hundred twenty?

Yeshivah University is playing football against Notre Dame. After the first quarter, the score is 56–0, favor of the Fighting Irish. The Yeshivah team decides to call its signals in Yiddish. (You can tell how old this joke is!)

The quarterback hunkers down and intones, "Dray-un-tsvantsik, zibn un fertsik, nayn un fuftsik …"[20]

From behind the Notre Dame lines comes a voice: "S'vet aykh gornisht helfn, kinderlekh!"[21]

Shnayder, a pious Jew and, in fact, himself a former shnayder (a tailor), is just not making it in his clothing store on the Lower East Side. He gets down on his knees and prays, "Got,[22] please help me make a living. You know I serve you faithfully. Can't you give me a break?"

The heavens part, and God answers, "It shall be done! You and I will be partners. From now on, success will be your lot."

Indeed, the store begins flourishing. Shnayder, enormously grateful and more than a little proud, actually changes its name from Shnayder's to Got un[23] Shnayder's. Business is so good that Shnayder decides to move to larger space uptown. He drops to his knees for another business consultation.

"Got, we're doing so well, I've decided to move up to Fifth Avenue."

The heavens part, and God answers, "Fine, but do you think Got un Shnayder's is a good name for a Fifth Avenue boutique?"

"I've been thinking about that," says Shnayder. "Why don't we just translate and call it Lord and Taylor's?"

Here is a classic story of the habitué of a famous Jewish restaurant, who finds a Chinese waiter taking his order in Yiddish one day:

> The customer calls the owner over and asks, "What gives? Where'd you find a Chinese guy who speaks Yiddish?"
>
> "Sha," the owner whispers, "he thinks we're teaching him English!"

---

20. Twenty-three, forty-seven, fifty-nine
21. It's not gonna help you, kids!
22. God
23. And

BILINGUAL AND MULTILINGUAL JOKES

The confluence of socioeconomic class and ethnicity is not a new phenomenon:

> In a second-class carriage on a train in the old country sit Russians eating onions, Poles eating radishes, and Jews eating garlic. A German countess accidentally wanders in from first class, takes one sniff, cries "Ach tfui!" and backs quickly out of the car.
> Following her is a Russian landowner, who, equally appalled, claps his hand over his nose, mutters "Ekh, bozhe moi!"[1] and heads back to first class.
> In their wake comes a little Jew. He opens the door, looks around, sniffs deeply, and says, "Ay, s'iz yontevdik!"[2]

Nor are assimilation and social climbing anything new. But Yiddish inevitably trips up the pretentious.

> A well-to-do Jewish family in the old country sends its daughter to the best schools in Europe. She comes home well-educated and with a fine Jewish husband as well. After a year, she finds herself in labor. The family calls their local doctor. The young mother-to-be is upstairs while the doctor sips tea in the parlor with husband and parents.
> Suddenly, there comes a cry from above, "O, mon Dieu, mon Dieu!"
> The family looks anxiously at the old doctor, who sips his tea, smiles, and says, "Not yet."
> "Ach du lieber Gott!" is heard from above. Again, the doctor doesn't move.
> "Oh my dear God!" comes the cry.
> "Not yet," says the doctor.
> After a short time, "Oy, vey iz mir, gotenyu mayner!"[3] is heard.
> "Now," says the doctor and hurries upstairs.

---

1. My God! (Russian)
2. It's like a holiday!
3. O woe is me, my dear God. (Yiddish)

Here's the latest incarnation of an oft-told tale about Jews who try to pass:

Madeleine Albright is invited to speak to a church group in Washington. She ascends the podium, puts on her glasses, and solemnly intones, "My fellow goyim …"

The nouveau riche Minnie Kaplan changes her name to Marilyn Carruthers, gets her hair and nose straightened, and joins the WASP country club. At the first ham and eggs brunch, she accidentally spills coffee on herself.
"Oy gevald!"[4] she cries. "Whatever that means."

Levy is trying to get into the restricted Bay Shores Country Club. He is denied admittance at the front desk, but he happens to glance at the members' registry and sees the name Cone. Not fooled for a minute by the spelling, Levy steps outside to the nearest phone, looks up Cone in the directory, and places the call.
"Hello, Cone residence, Mr. Cone speaking," intones a patrician voice.
"My name is Levy, and I'd like to know how you, as a Jew, got into the Bay Shores Country Club."
"Sir, I am affronted by your call," replies Cone, "and I am appalled by your presumption. I am an Episcopalian. My father is an Episcopalian. And my grandfather, olev hasholem,[5] was an Episcopalian."

A Jew from New York visits London. He is mightily impressed by Harrod's Department Store and finds himself in the prepared foods section attended by a clerk—tall, razor-thin, three-piece suit, pince-nez, and haughty manner to match.
"How may I help you?" asks the clerk.
"Well, I'd like a pound of cream cheese."
"Sir," intones the clerk, "Harrod's sells Emmenthaler. Harrod's sells Gruyere. Harrod's sells traditional English Cheddar, but Harrod's does not carry cream cheese."
"Okay, give me a pound of each of those. And how about two pounds of lox?"
The clerk pulls himself up even straighter. "Sir, Harrod's carries Scottish smoked salmon. Harrod's carries Greenland smoked salmon, but Harrod's certainly does not carry lox."
"Fine. I'll take a pound of those. And a dozen bagels."

---

4. Oh good grief.
5. The traditional Hebrew-Yiddish expression for "May he rest in peace."

The clerk peers over his pince-nez. "Sir, Harrod's has scones. Harrod's has croissants. Harrod's even has ecological multigrain breads. But Harrod's most certainly does not sell bagels."

"Fine, so put together a dozen of those. Could you bring it all out to my car?"

The clerk draws himself up to his full height and declares, "Sir, Harrod's does not shlep."[6]

An elderly Jewish lady in Miami goes to a travel agency and asks to book a trip to Nepal. The surprised travel agent gets her on a plane from Miami to Katmandu. Once out of Nepalese customs, she hails the nearest cab and says, "Take me to the Katmandu Lama."

"Madam, the Katmandu Lama lives in a cave on top of a mountain, surrounded by Sherpa guards. He hardly ever sees anyone."

"So, get me to the nearest town and hire me a guide. I gotta see the Lama."

The cab drops her at the foot of the mountain. A guide takes her to the entrance of the cave, where two burly Sherpas block her entrance.

"Please," she says, "I'm an old lady. I came all the way from Miami. I need to say three words to the Katmandu Lama."

The Sherpas relay her message and return. "The Lama has agreed to see you on the condition you only say three words, no more."

"Agreed."

She enters the cave, where the Lama is sitting cross-legged on a woven rug and intoning a mantra. She approaches him.

As he looks up, she says, "Sheldon, shoyn genug!"[7]

In Czarist Russia, four Jewish converts to Christianity are discussing their motives.

The first says, "I wanted to be a professor at the university, not a melamed in a kheder. So I converted."

The second explains, "I had a love affair with a Russian girl. The family caught us and offered me the choice of converting and marrying her or being killed on the spot. So I became a Christian."

The third says, "I'm ashamed to admit it, but I'm a thief. The authorities caught me and told me I could either go to jail or convert. So I did the obvious thing."

---

6. Tote; carry. A very slangy Yiddish word.
7. Enough already!

The fourth fellow states with pride, "I became a Christian because I believe in the divinity of Christ, the virgin birth, and the Holy Trinity."

"Feh!" shout the other three. "Gey dertseyl dos di goyim!"[8]

Note how this joke would not be funny at all if the punch line was not in Yiddish. In particular, the term "goyim" in this context is not neutral, as it was in the Albright story above. It has a bite here, which the neutral translation "Gentiles" absolutely fails to convey.

In a similar vein:

A devoutly Catholic reporter dies and is admitted into heaven. Because he was a good and religious man, St. Peter offers him any one wish. He asks for an exclusive interview with the Virgin Mary.

Escorted into her presence, he kneels before her and asks, "Holy Mother, how did you feel when you learned you were chosen to give birth to the Son of God?"

Mary smiles ruefully and replies, "Ikh hob azoy gevolt a meydele!"[9]

Here, an English punch line might be mildly amusing at best. Making Mary into an East European Jewish mother is what gives the joke its charm.

A sly comment on Christian anti-Semitism:

Two beggars stand outside of a church on a Sunday morning. One wears a Jewish star, and the other wears a cross. The congregants leaving the church shun the former. For spite, they reward the latter richly with coins and bills. The pastor, seeing this display of bigotry, approaches the beggar with the star and says, "Look, my man, you can see my flock is not behaving in the most Christian manner. But there's a synagogue just two streets away. Why not go over there and beg?"

The beggar looks at the pastor and calls over to the other beggar, "Moishe, ze ver lernt unds gesheft!"[10]

Sometimes, the stories have no particular message. It's just the language element itself providing the source of laughter.

---

8. Tell that one to the Gentiles!
9. I really wanted a little girl.
10. Moishe, look who's teaching us about business!

> In a trial in Boston, the next witness is called—Rabbi Abraham Goldstein. In marches a Hassid in full regalia: beard, peyes, kapote, and yarmulke. The judge takes one look and tells the bailiff, "Get the Jewish interpreter."
> The interpreter approaches the witness, just as the bailiff swears him in, "State your name, age, and occupation."
> Before the interpreter can open his mouth, the Hassid replies in perfect Oxonian English, "Rabbi Dr. Abraham Goldstein, fifty-two years of age, Professor of Comparative Literature, Harvard University."
> The interpreter announces to the court, "Zayn nomen is Harov Dokter Avrum Goldshteyn, er is tsvey un fuftsik yor alt, un iz a professor fun farglaykhiker literatur in Harvard."

Here are two vulgar little tales that share a common theme and only work with the punch line in Yiddish. I couldn't tell you why.

> One night, a Jew gets so drunk that he wanders out of the town and goes up to the cemetery, where he falls unconscious into a freshly dug grave. The morning sun awakens him. He looks around, mystified as to his whereabouts. Finally, he decides to think it through Talmudically.
> "If I see the sky above me, then I must be lying down. If I'm lying down and see earth on all four sides around me, then I must be in a grave. If I'm in a grave, then I must be dead. But, if I'm dead, to voshze darf ikh azoy pishn?"[11]

> Konstantin Petrovich Pobedonostsev, the anti-Semitic adviser to Czars Alexander III and Nicholas II, is reputed to have presided over a urinating contest in the Pale of Settlement. Any Jew who could "write" Pobedonostsev's long name in the sand would be granted the right to live in Moscow. (What's second prize, you ask? But let's go on.)
> Several try and fail. Finally, one little Jew comes forward and says, "I'll give it a shot, but I need one of your soldiers to, so to speak, direct the stream."
> Pobedonostsev is surprised at the request, but he directs a soldier to assist the contestant. To the amazement of the assembled, the Jew is not only able to sustain enough "ink" for Pobedonostsev, but even for a fancy little underline.
> "Remarkable," says Pobedonostsev. "But tell me the truth, why did you ask that my soldier hold your implement?"
> The Jew blushes. "Pishn ken ikh; shraybn ken ikh nisht!"[12]

---

11. So why do I have to pee so badly?
12. I know how to pee; I don't know how to write!

Two New York Jews, Abe and Moishe, are visiting Santa Fe. They come upon an Indian selling handwoven blankets.
"How much?" asks Abe.
"Twenty dollar," replies the Indian.
Moishe nudges Abe and says, "S'iz gornit vert tsvantsik doler; gib im tsen."[13]
To which, the Indian replies, "Hot rakhmones: ikh hob aleyn batsolt tsvelf."[14]

Jews from Bialystok in eastern Poland are inordinately proud of their town, sometimes to excess.

A Bialystoker Jew is invited for a summer visit by his relatives in New York City. First, they take him to Coney Island on the Fourth of July. More than a million people are on the beach. The Bialystoker looks around unimpressed and says, "Dos hobn mir oykh in Bialystok."[15]
They take him to the top of the Empire State Building. He gazes out the window and again says, "Dos hobn mir oykh in Bialystok."
At wit's end, the New York relatives take him into the heart of Chinatown to a restaurant filled with Chinese patrons. The menu is entirely in Chinese. The Chinese waiter is standing patiently to take the order. The Bialystoker looks around, looks at the menu, and finally confesses, "Dos hobn mir nit in Bialystok."[16]
The waiter bursts out, "Ir zent oykh a Bialystoker?"[17]

A Jew comes to America in the Roaring Twenties. He goes directly to Chicago, where the Hebrew Immigrant Aid Society has found him an apartment and a job. No sooner does he get off the train and into the street, than a limousine roars past him with men in black shirts, white ties, and grey fedoras firing Tommy guns at a pursuing police car. From the limousine is thrown a suitcase, landing at the feet of the new immigrant. He opens it, looks in, and sees it is bursting with money.
"Ay, America, America, truly a golden land," he declares. Putting the suitcase under his arm, he goes to find his new apartment.

---

13. It's not worth twenty dollars; give him ten.
14. Have a heart; I paid twelve myself.
15. This we also have in Bialystok.
16. This we *don't* have in Bialystok.
17. You're also a Bialystoker!

Two days later, well-installed, he is surprised by a knock on the door. He opens it and sees two men in black shirts, white ties, and grey fedoras.

"Give us our money."

The Jew replies, "Ikh farshtey nisht."[18]

The men leave, returning a half hour later with a Yiddish-speaking rabbi.

"Tell him we want our money."

The rabbi translates.

The immigrant thinks, "No way I'm parting with $100,000."

"Ikh farshtey nisht."

The rabbi translates, "He says he doesn't understand."

The two hoods reply, "Tell him we'll break both his arms if he doesn't give us the money."

The rabbi translates.

The immigrant thinks, "$100,000 is certainly worth two broken arms."

He again tells the rabbi, "Ikh farshtey nisht."

The rabbi translates, "He says he still doesn't understand."

The two hoods reply, "Tell him we'll break both his legs if he doesn't give us the money."

The rabbi dutifully translates.

The immigrant thinks, "$100,000 is even worth two broken arms and two broken legs."

He again tells the rabbi, "Ikh farshtey nisht."

The rabbi translates, "He says he still doesn't understand."

The two hoods reply, "Tell him we'll kill him if he doesn't give us the money."

The rabbi translates.

The immigrant thinks, "$100,000 is certainly not worth dying for."

He tells the rabbi, "Dos gelt is untern bet."[19]

The rabbi turns to the two thugs. "He says he still doesn't understand."

---

18. I don't understand.
19. The money is under the bed.

JOKES THAT DO, ALMOST DO, AND DO NOT TRANSLATE

We've already had a good example of a joke that works in Yiddish but not in English, the kheyder boy who tells his teacher "Ikh hob dir in drerd." It also works in French, which has both a polite and informal "you," but not in Hebrew, which doesn't. Languages sometimes have common expressions, so jokes translate easily. Sometimes, as in this case, they don't at all. Moreover, some are somewhere in between. Here are examples of all three.

Jokes That Do

In the Old Country, students studying at yeshivahs far from home were often fed by Jewish families in the yeshivah town—a different family every day (if they were lucky enough to get fed every day). The custom was called *esn teg* (eating days).

> In one such yeshivah town there arrives a young scholar, a reputed genius. The more prominent families immediately seek him as a dinner guest. On the first Sunday, he is served baked beans by the baleboste.[1] Baked beans happen to be his favorite dish, and he eats them with much gusto.
> The baleboste, very pleased, tells the next evening's hostess, who also prepares baked beans. The student eats them, but with a shade less enthusiasm.
> And so it goes, from house to house, until Thursday evening, he is served his fifth consecutive baked beans dinner. He simply stares at the plate.
> With some concern, the baleboste asks him, "Why aren't you eating? I understood you liked baked beans."
> "Indeed I do," replies the student. "But unfortunately, I can't eat them because I don't know the appropriate brokhe[2] to say over them."
> "What brokhe? Is there a special brokhe?" asks the worried hostess.

---

1. Woman of the house. Pronounced bah-leh-BOS-teh.
2. Blessing

"Well," replies the yeshiva student, "when it comes from the ground, I know the brokhe. When it comes from the sea, I know the brokhe. When it comes from a vine, I know the brokhe. But I just don't know the brokhe when it's coming out of my ears!"

The Yiddish original is "Ven se krikht mir shoyn fun haldz aroys (When it's coming up out of my throat already)," but the English expression works perfectly well.

A Jew comes to a strange town, looking for Mr. Goldberg, the synagogue president. The first Jew he asks says, "Goldberg? That scoundrel, I spit on him!"
The Jew asks another, who replies, "Goldberg, that mamzer! I wouldn't give him the time of day!"
And so it goes, one after another, until the Jew finally finds Mr. Goldberg.
"Tell me, Mr. Goldberg, why are you willing to serve as the president of the synagogue?"
"For the koved."³

Two elderly Jewish ladies are visiting the Jewish cemetery in Paris. They come upon the Rothschild family mausoleum—huge, engraved marble with gilt edging, and surrounded by freshly cut flowers.
One turns to the other and says, "Dos heyst gelebt!"⁴

Jokes that Almost Do, But Not Quite

A shatkhn comes to a prospective bridegroom. "Have I got a bride for you! Beautiful, intelligent, educated, and from a wealthy family."
"What's her name?"
"Rivkeh, the daughter of Yankl of Plotsk."
"Her?" says the young man. "I've heard she's slept with half the men in Plotsk."
The shatkhn replies, "Plotsk, oykh mir a shtot!"⁵

The humor ostensibly stems from the shatkhn's minimizing of the girl's promiscuity by denigrating the size of Plotsk. That comes through in the English. That is not quite what is connoted in the original Yiddish. "Plotsk, oykh mir a

---

3. Honor
4. That's living!
5. Plotsk, you call that a city?

shtot" in fact shifts the entire discussion away from the girl's behavior and onto the provinciality of the town itself. The shatkhn's pretense is that the young man is criticizing the town, not the girl. The source of humor here is the inventiveness of the shatkhn, based on a sense of competition among East European Jews vis-à-vis their towns.

Jews in Eastern Europe had various legendary pranksters, about whom comic tales were told. Each region had its own. The Litvak prankster was Motke Chabad.

> One Shabbes afternoon, the Jews are sitting in the synagogue yard, discussing philosophical and theological issues. The topic turns, as it sometimes does, to death. One of the Jews announces, "I would like to lie next to Reb Moishe, of blessed memory, the greatest scholar our town ever produced."
> A second Jew professes, "I would like to lie next to Yossele, the water carrier, may he rest in peace. Although a simple man, he was truly one of the righteous of the earth."
> And so the conversation goes on. Finally, only Motke is left.
> "Nu, Motke, and you?"
> Motke replies, "I would like to lie next to Rokhele, the daughter of Opatov, the richest man in our town."
> "What are you saying, Motke? She's not dead!"
> "So what am I, a corpse?"

The joke is funny enough in translation, but the Yiddish has an extra little kick. Just as there are several words for die, so are there several words for corpse, of varying degrees of elegance or lack of same. In the original, Motke says, "Toh vos bin ikh, a peyger?" choosing the coarsest, peyger, usually referring to an animal. The juxtaposition of this with the preceding high-toned discussion adds to the humor of the sexual allusion.

Here is a popular story told in both Yiddish and English. Let's compare and contrast. The English version:

> A synagogue is looking for a new cantor. They receive an application from the cantor of a neighboring synagogue. With the application is a fine letter of recommendation from his rabbi, "Our cantor is a combination of Moses, Shakespeare, and Einstein."
> The cantor is auditioned and turns out to be awful—both professionally and personally.

> The rabbi writes angrily to his colleague at the synagogue, where the cantor is currently employed.
> "Apparently, you are trying to get rid of him, and I can well see why. But how could you lie so baldly in your letter of recommendation?"
> He receives a reply, "I didn't lie at all. Moses stammered, so does the cantor. Shakespeare couldn't read Hebrew, neither can he. And Einstein couldn't carry a tune!"

Putting aside the fact that Einstein was an accomplished violinist, let's look at the Yiddish version:

> The recommendation says, "Our cantor is a combination of Moishe Rabbenu [Moses], the Baal Shem [founder of Hassidism], and God."
> The reply to the rabbi says, "Moishe stammered, so does the cantor. The Baal Shem couldn't sing, neither can he. And God is not a mentsh, nor is the cantor."

The substitution of the Baal Shem and God for Shakespeare and Einstein keeps the context entirely Jewish. (Actually, of course, the substitution went the other way. The Yiddish original was modified so that English speakers, many of whom had never heard of the Baal Shem, would get it.) But why God? Because the word "mentsh" has a double entendre. Literally, it means human being. So God is not a mentsh. But the phrase "not a mentsh," when applied to a person, means of low character and mean-spirited. It is something like the English, "not fit to be in a room with other human beings."

Jokes that Just Don't

These can be told in Yiddish or English with the punch line in Yiddish, which I shall do. But they simply do not translate. Sometimes the critical words don't have an English equivalent. Mostly, it's because the concepts expressed exist only in Yiddish.

> Two Jewish ladies meet on the street.
> "So how's your daughter?" asks the one.
> "Well," replies the other, "she married a doctor."
> "A doctor? How wonderful!"
> "Well, but she divorced him and married a lawyer."
> "Nu, a lawyer! How nice."
> "Yeh, but she then divorced him. Now she's married to an accountant."

"Ay," replies the other, "A doctor, a lawyer, and a CPA, so much nakhes from one daughter!"

Nakhes is a unique type of pleasure derived vicariously from the accomplishments of one's children. I know of no single-word equivalent in English.

> The widower Cohen asks the widow Feldman if she would like to share a two-bedroom apartment with him. Just to save money, no ulterior motives. Because they're both retired and on fixed incomes, she accepts. Six months later, she's having lunch with her friend Mrs. Sheinberg, who asks her how it's working out.
> "Better than I expected. For the first month, we pretty well kept to ourselves. But one evening, there was a knock on my bedroom door, and there was Mr. Cohen with a bottle of champagne. 'My granddaughter just graduated from college, summa cum laude. Would you like to celebrate with me?' So I said sure. One drink led to another. One thing led to another. The next thing I know, we were intimate. Several weeks later, again a knock. Again there he is with the champagne. 'My grandson just graduated from law school. Would you like to share in my joy?' So I did, and the same thing happened. Then just last week, a knock … a bottle of champagne. 'My other granddaughter just finished medical school.' So we celebrated in the usual way. I tell you, I am getting such nakhes from his grandchildren!"

> A Jew goes to his tailor with a bolt of cloth to have a suit made. The tailor takes the measurements and tells him to return in a week.
> When he tries on the suit, one sleeve is longer than the other.
> "Hold your shoulder up like so, and no one will notice," says the tailor.
> But one leg is also longer than the other.
> "Bend your knee a little, and then they'll match."
> Then it appears the jacket is a little shorter on one side.
> "Just tilt your body a bit, and it'll look fine."
> The Jew leaves the shop and is walking down the street when a stranger stops him. "Who's your tailor? I must see him!"
> "Why?"
> "Because," says the stranger, "anyone who can fit a kalike like you must be a genius."

Kalike translates literally as "cripple." But using cripple in the joke renders it not the slightest bit funny. In fact, it comes across as offensive. Kalike has a jovial connotation, which cripple entirely lacks.

> When Arthur Miller married Marilyn Monroe, one Jew predicted, "It won't last a year." To which, his friend replied, "Aza yor of mir!"

Aza yor of mir translates literally as "such a year on me," which is not funny because English has no such expression. However, it is a most common one in Yiddish and is usually used seriously to wish things should get better for one. The use of it to wish for Marilyn Monroe is a charming example of Jewish acculturation in America.

This next one uses an expression that (I think) only exists in Yiddish:

> Shortly after the formation of the State of Israel, David Ben Gurion, its first prime minister, is on a fund-raising tour of America. He's approached by a wealthy American Jew, who says, "I'll give you a million dollars if you make me a minister of state."
> "Sorry," says Ben Gurion, "governmental positions are not for sale."
> "How about two million?"
> "Let me get back to you," says the prime minister.
> Six months later, Ben Gruion returns to the United States for another fundraiser. And there's the wealthy Jew again.
> "So what about my offer?"
> "I've talked it over with the Knesset," says Ben Gurion, "and, for two million dollars, we are ready to offer you, not one, but two ministries."
> "Wow! Which ones?"
> "The Ministry of Health and the Ministry of Tourism."
> "Great! What are my responsibilities?"
> "You have an office at the top of the lighthouse tower in Haifa harbor. Whenever a ship leaves port, you stick your head out the window and yell, 'For gezunt un kum gezunt!'"[6]

To give English its due, reverse translation doesn't always work either. One of the favorite playwrights of Yiddish-speaking immigrants was none other than William Shakespeare. The Bard was promptly translated into Yiddish, with one newspaper proudly announcing, "Shakespeare, fartaytsht un farbesert" (Shakes-

---

6. "Go in good health and return in good health." A traditional Yiddish wish for travelers.

peare, translated and improved). The plays were performed to adoring audiences. Why were they so popular? The original words are certainly English, but Jews found many of the tunes familiar. *King Lear*, the story of a doting parent with ungrateful children, was far and away the most popular play on the Yiddish stage. In fact, a story is told about the classic American actor Louis Calhern, who gets in a cab in New York City one morning and asks to be taken to the Schubert Theater on Broadway.

> The Jewish cabbie recognizes him and asks what play he is rehearsing.
> "*King Lear*," replies Calhern.
> The cabbie asks, "You think it'll work in English?"

Unlike the original, the *Jewish King Lear* (yes, that was its title) does not have his eyes plucked out. He goes blind from an illness while visiting the Holy Land. Perhaps Jews found the original violence too goyish. But then, how do we account for the immense popularity of the very goyish *Hamlet* with opening night audiences shouting, "Author! Author!" (The lead player finally told them the author couldn't be there because he was in England.)

This leads us to what is arguably the most idiosyncratic translation of all time, the opening of Hamlet's soliloquy, "Zayn oder nit zayn: do ligt der hunt bagrobn." (To be or not to be: that's where the dog lies buried.)

While we're talking Shakespeare, this one maybe doesn't belong in Language Humor, but I can't resist.

> The Royal Shakespeare Repertory Company is traveling around the world, looking for a new leading man. No luck. Nowhere is there anyone of the stature of, say, the late, great Olivier. Finally, they end up in New York. For three weeks, they audition hopefuls, but no one can quite cut it.
> The Company is about to pack up on the last day when a knock comes on the stage door, and in walks a little Jew.
> "Vould it be okay if I take a shot?" he asks in heavily accented Yinglish.
> The Company is dubious, but what's there to lose? A little comic relief would be nice.
> "I'm gonna do Hemlet's solilokvy," says the Jew. With that, he launches into "To be or not to be ..." in fluent British English, letter-perfect, from memory, and with a brilliant interpretation.
> The Company is on its feet with applause, and he is hired on the spot. The director takes him aside and can't resist asking, "I hear how you talk nor-

mally. How in the world are you able to do Shakespeare without a trace of accent?"

The Jew pulls himself up, smiles broadly, points his finger at the director, and says "Det's ecting!"

Part Four
NONE OF THE ABOVE

In this, the final section of the book, we turn to jokes that don't fit into the above categories of laughing inward, laughing outward, or language humor. Maybe some of them do, but I like them better in other categories. I hope you'll agree. But maybe not. Whatever.

COMPARE AND CONTRAST—JEWISH/NON-JEWISH VARIANTS

Many stories told as Jewish jokes turn up with some variation in other contexts—Catholic jokes, blond jokes, computer jokes, to name only three. Is there, in fact, nothing specifically Jewish about such jokes? Or is there something in the variations themselves that changes the meaning? Both situations occur, depending on the particular story.

Let's start off with those stories that are told by members of different religions and see how they are similar and, if in some ways, different.

> A wealthy congregant comes to his rabbi and asks him to perform the eulogy for his lately deceased dog. The rabbi refuses.
> "I am a clergyman. I don't perform funeral rites over animals."
> The congregant offers the rabbi $20,000 for the synagogue building fund.
> At the pet cemetery the very next day, one congregant says to the other, "What a eulogy the rabbi gave. I had no idea that dog was such a friend of Israel!"

In the Catholic version, the priest initially refuses, but, when the congregant offers the $20,000, he immediately responds with, "Of course. Why didn't you tell me Rover was a devout Catholic?" Except for the details, these jokes are the same in every way. This is not surprising because they reflect an American reality, the private funding of religious institutions.

Now let's look at another story told in both a Jewish and a Catholic version. The Jewish version:

> The bar mitzvah service had gone off without a hitch. The boy made a fine speech in which he promised to be a faithful, observant Jew, go to daily

> prayer at the synagogue, put on tefillin each morning, and so on. His parents invite all their friends over for the bar mitzvah banquet. Of course, they also invite the rabbi. For the occasion, they put out their best silver.
> After the guests have left, they notice a spoon is missing. "It couldn't have been one of our friends. That rabbi must be the thief." They resign from the synagogue and never talk to the rabbi again.
> Some five years later, the son encounters the rabbi in town. He decides to have the issue out ... then and there.
> "You know, Rabbi, the reason we quit the synagogue was a silver spoon was missing after my bar mitzvah banquet, and the family was forced to conclude you must have taken it."
> "I assumed that is what they had assumed," replies the rabbi. "Why don't you look in your tefillin bag?"

Here's the Catholic version:

> A young priest, newly arrived in the parish, is invited to dinner at the lodging of the old priest. When the newcomer arrives, he is surprised to note the old priest has a beautiful, young housekeeper. The old priest notices his surprise and remarks, "Whatever you are thinking is not the case. I sleep in my bedroom upstairs, and she sleeps in the bedroom off the kitchen."
> After the conclusion of dinner and a pleasant evening, the young priest takes his leave.
> The next day, the housekeeper says, "There seems to be a spoon missing."
> The old priest assures her that he will handle it as diplomatically as possible. He calls his young colleague and says, "No one is accusing anyone of anything, but my housekeeper tells me a spoon is missing."
> To which, the young priest replies, "No one is accusing anyone of anything, but did you look on your pillow?"

Same joke? Well, almost. The rabbi has called the youth to account for his failure to observe the law requiring the wearing of tefillin, and the young priest has accused his older colleague of violating the law of celibacy. And yet, while both versions deal with hypocrisy, the Jewish one has a certain moralistic tone, a preachiness to it. The Catholic one is earthier, and I think funnier.

Here's one where the wording is identical, except fill in the blank with Catholic or Jewish:

> A _____ girl leaves home at eighteen to make her way in the world. Three years later, she returns, driving a Rolls Royce and dressed in the latest Paris fashions. Her mother greets her with joy and says, "You certainly have done well! I'm so proud of you."
> The girl blushes and replies, "Mama, maybe you shouldn't be so proud. I've become a prostitute."
> "Oh my God, how awful! I'm so ashamed. How can I live with this? What will our family and friends think?"
> "Well," says the daughter, "you don't have to tell them I'm a prostitute."
> The mother's face is suddenly wreathed in smiles. "Did you say a prostitute? Thank God! I thought you said a Protestant!"

Is it the same joke for both? Again, almost. In both cases, we might say selling your body is eminently preferable to selling your soul. But, in the Jewish version, it's primarily the wordplay providing the humor. In the Catholic version, the knife goes deeper. Anything is better than being a Protestant.

Here's one that truly is the same, although the main characters are different. The Jewish version:

> The Pope, the Dalai Lama, and the Lubavitcher Rebbe, the leader of the largest Hassidic sect, die and go to heaven. God decides to greet them. They come into a large room, and there is the Lord, sitting on a beautiful throne. He turns to the Pope and says, "Tell me about your life on earth."
> The Pope replies, "I was the spiritual leader of millions of Catholics. I believe I led them in the ways of righteousness and taught them to love thy holy name."
> "Indeed you did," says God. "Come sit here on my right side."
> He then asks the Dalai Lama about his time on earth.
> "I led the Tibetan people as best I could. I struggled on their behalf, and I taught them to serve you in our way."
> "Indeed you did. Come sit on my left."
> He asks the Rebbe, "And you?"
> "I led the worldwide movement of Lubavitcher Hassidim … and you're in my chair."

There are (at least) three variants of this, with different characters displaying their hubris.

The Zionist version:

> David Ben Gurion, Chaim Weizmann, and Menachem Begin are sitting around in heaven, and they begin discussing politics. God soon joins in and proves quite knowledgeable.
> Weizmann says, "Why don't we form a political discussion society?"
> "Okay," says Ben Gurion, "I'll be the president."

The physicists' version:

> Albert Einstein, Enrico Fermi, and Niels Bohr are sitting around in heaven, and they begin discussing quantum mechanics. God soon joins in and proves quite knowledgeable.
> Einstein says, "Why don't we form a research group?"
> "Okay," says Fermi, "I'll be the leader."

The Catholic version:

> The Pope realizes he will soon die and calls in his trusted aide.
> "I know my earthly days are numbered. I should like to be buried in a place and a fashion that will make my memory immortal."
> "Why not right here in St. Peter's, like your predecessors?" suggests the aide.
> "Not good enough. My predecessors did not achieve my stature."
> "Well, how about somewhere in the Holy Land?"
> "Wonderful idea! I should like to be buried in Christ's tomb in Jerusalem. Call up the Israeli government and see to the arrangements."
> The aide returns shortly with the response. "The Israelis say it's fine. The arrangements will cost $50,000."
> "Hmm," muses the Pope, "isn't that a little steep for just two nights?"

Here's one that is virtually identical in both wording and intent:

> A Jew dies and goes to heaven. He's greeted by the Angel Gabriel, who asks which section he'd like to be housed in: Reform, Conservative, or Orthodox.
> "Let me have a look at all three."
> Gabriel takes him first to the Reform section. He opens a large door into an auditorium where bareheaded rabbis are discussing with their congregants whether there is enough social action content in their heavenly behavior.

They move on to the Conservative section. Here is an auditorium full of men and women, sitting together and arguing about whether they are violating Halakhic Law by doing so.
Finally, they approach the Orthodox section. As he opens the door, Gabriel cautions the Jew, "Be absolutely quiet when you look in."
"Why?"
"Because they think they're the only ones up here!"

In the Catholic version, just substitute Presbyterians for Reform Jews, Anglicans for Conservative Jews, and Catholics, of course, for Orthodox Jews.

This time, I will present the Catholic version first:

A Jew decides to convert to Catholicism. Part of the procedure is baptism.
"From your experience, what is appropriate for me to wear?" the Jew asks a Catholic friend.
"From my experience, a white dress with woolen booties would do just fine!"

The Jewish version:

A Catholic decides to convert to Judaism. Part of the procedure is circumcision.
"Is it very painful?" the Catholic asks a Jewish friend.
"Painful? I couldn't walk for a year!"

What about the same stories in different cultures? Some stories that travel well are those in which, not only is the situation the same, but the reaction of the protagonists is the same.

Maurie makes it big in the Big Apple. He wants to send his mother in Miami a really elegant birthday gift. For $1,000, he purchases a talking bird. But it's not just any talking bird. This one speaks English, Yiddish, Hebrew, French, and Spanish.
He has the bird sent to his mother and calls her the next day. "So, Mama, what'd you think of the bird?"
"Delicious," replies his mother.
"You ate it! Mama, that bird spoke five languages!"
"So why didn't it say something when I put it in the pot?"

The exact same story is told by New Orleans Cajuns. Maurie becomes Beauregard, and Miami is changed to the Bayou. Why does it work? Like Jews, younger, educated Cajuns have overcome the privations suffered by their parents. And, like Jews, Cajuns are ready to poke fun at the pretensions of parvenu children.

> A Pole sitting on a train asks a Jew, "How come you people are so smart?"
> "Fish heads," replies the Jew. "We eat them. I happen to have one here, which I'll sell you for ten zlotys."
> "Okay," says the Pole. He gives the Jew the money and proceeds to devour the fish head. Just then, a hawker comes through the train, selling fish heads for five zlotys.
> "Hey," says the Pole, "that's half what you charged me!"
> "You see?" says the Jew. "It's working."

Bengalis tell a very similar joke about themselves and Sikhs. In Indian culture, fish heads are a delicacy.

> A Sikh asks a Bengali, "How come you people are so smart?"
> The Bengali says, "We eat specially prepared fish. Buy a fish every day, and I'll prepare it in the special way that makes us smart."
> The Sikh makes the daily purchase, and the Bengali prepares it, gives the body to the Sikh, and keeps the head for himself.
> After several weeks, the Sikh says, "How come I only get the body and you always get the head?"
> The Bengali answers, "See, it's working."

It is worth examining in some detail the difference between these two ostensibly similar stories. Sikhs and Bengalis each have regions within India in which they are the majority. The popular stereotype of the Sikh is a laborer, that of the Bengali is an intellectual. The question, "How come you people are so smart?" from a Sikh to a Bengali is emotionally neutral. It could as easily be rendered, "How come you people are so intelligent?" Therefore, according to my Indian informant, the story is simply making fun of the purported stupidity of Sikhs. It's a negative ethnic joke, like American Polish jokes.

Is that all the Jewish version is? I don't think so. The Jews who invented this joke were living as a perpetual minority in a Polish culture that was not only Christian, but often virulently anti-Semitic. The words, "How come you people are so smart?" from the Pole have a sting to Jewish ears. They suggest not intelligence, but craftiness and cunning. The Jewish version is attacking not a Pole per se, but an anti-Semite. Different cultures, different codes.

Speaking of anti-Semitism, the next example shows how a traditional American Jewish joke that Jews tell each other has been "anti-Semitized." The Jewish version is first:

> A Jewish husband and wife are having dinner at a restaurant when the wife spies an absolutely stunning young woman at another table and asks her husband, "Who's that?"
> "Oh," replies the husband, "she's my mistress."
> "You have a mistress? Does anyone else we know have one?"
> "Yes, Moishe does. She's the woman sitting at that other table over there."
> The wife says, "I like ours better."

The joke is the charming naïveté and loyalty of the Jewish wife. It was the basis of a scene in Neil Simon's *California Suite*. Here's the Internet version, ominously titled, "Who says money can't buy love?":

> A Jewish husband and wife were having dinner at a very fine restaurant when this absolutely stunning young woman comes over to their table and gives the husband a big open-mouthed kiss. Then she says she'll see him later and walks away.
> The wife glares at her husband and says, "Who the hell was that?"
> "Oh," replies the husband, "she's my mistress."
> "Well, that's the last straw," says the wife. "I've had enough. I want a divorce!"
> "I can understand that," replies her husband. "Remember, if we get a divorce, it will mean no more shopping trips to Paris, no more wintering in Barbados, no more summers in Tuscany, no more BMW in the garage, and no more yacht club. But the decision is yours."
> Just then, a mutual friend enters the restaurant with a gorgeous babe on his arm.
> "Who's that woman with Moishe?" asks the wife.
> "That's his mistress," says her husband.
> "Ours is prettier," she replies.

As my late mother would say, "Feh!"

Rigid adherence to rules is a trait ascribed both to the English and to Yeckes.

> Six men are marooned on a desert island for a year: two Welshmen, two Scots, and two Englishmen. At the end of the year, a ship rescues them. During their ordeal, the two Welshmen have formed a choir. The two Scots have

founded a distillery. The Englishmen haven't spoken to each other. They hadn't been properly introduced.

Now the Jewish variant:

> A Yecke buys a train ticket. "I want a seat by the window, facing the direction of motion of the train." The conductor sells him the ticket.
> After the three-hour ride, the Yecke, about to disembark, upbraids the conductor, "This was an awful trip. My assigned seat was away from the window and opposite to the direction of motion."
> "I'm terribly sorry for the error, sir, but couldn't you just ask the other person to change seats?"
> "Quite impossible," sniffs the Yecke. "I was alone in the compartment."

Here's more comparative humor among various cultures. The English version:

> Nigel comes home early from work to find his wife in bed with Trevor, his best friend.
> "Trevor, I must say. I am surprised."
> Trevor replies, "Indeed not, Nigel. It is I who am surprised. You are astonished."

There's also a version told by Danes, for whom hospitality is everything:

> Ole comes home early from work to find his wife in bed with Lasse, his best friend. From behind Lasse's back, Ole motions to his wife. "Get rid of him. We only have two beers in the fridge."

Now, here's one Jewish version:

> Hyman comes home early from work to find his wife in bed with Moishe, his best friend.
> "Moishe," he says, "I have to. But you?"

Here's another:

> Hyman comes home early from work to find his wife in bed with Moishe, his best friend.
> His wife looks up and says, "Watch. Learn something."

Here's the ultra-Orthodox Jewish version:

> Reb Yisroel comes home early to his apartment in Jerusalem and catches his wife Rivkeh in bed with his best friend.
> "What's next, Rivkeh?" he demands. "Smoking on Shabbes?"

Another type of story that travels well is the one concerning various ethnicities aboard a doomed airplane. Here's the Jewish version:

> A Frenchman, an Englishman, a German, and a Jew are on an airplane. The pilot announces they're losing fuel and will crash unless the plane is lightened, namely someone will have to jump to his death to save the others.
> The Frenchman cries, "Vive la France!" and jumps from the plane.
> But the plane continues losing fuel, and another sacrifice must be made.
> The Englishman cries, "God save the Queen!" and jumps.
> Again the pilot announces more weight must be jettisoned.
> So the Jew shouts, "Am Yisroel Chai!"[1] and throws the German out.

There are many versions of this, including one in which the German shouts, "Deutschland Über Alles" and throws the Jew out, giving the joke a very different tone and meaning. But a variant that comes fairly close to the Jewish one is the Scandinavian version. These nations boast of their close cooperation with one another and have, by no means, the history of Jews and Germans. Nevertheless, there is a residue of negative feeling toward the more populous, powerful Sweden. So:

> A Norwegian, a Dane, and a Swede are on an airplane. The pilot announces they're losing fuel and will crash unless the plane is lightened, namely someone will have to jump to his death to save the others.
> The Norwegian and the Dane cry, "Long live Scandinavian cooperation!" and throw the Swede out.

Another Jewish joke with a Scandinavian counterpart is the following, dating at least from the last century:

> Three students are asked to write an essay about the elephant. The English student writes, "The Elephant as a Mode of Travel in the British Colony of India." The French student writes, "The Love Life of the Elephant." The Jewish student writes, "The Elephant and the Jewish Question." ("The Jew-

---

1. The people of Israel lives

ish Question" referred to the minority position of Jews in all societies. Since the establishment of the State of Israel, it has effectively been removed from the agenda.)

What is the source of the humor? The first two, albeit parodied through the lens of their own nationality, at least relate the elephant to something it's ... well ... possible to relate to. The Jews, by their own account (this is after all a Jewish joke) were so concerned (obsessed with) "the Jewish question" they would relate anything to it.

The Scandinavian version is similar, although perhaps more extreme. It focuses on Norwegians, who purportedly feel misunderstood by all and sundry, so much so that this is the only topic on their minds. So:

> Asked to write an essay about the elephant, the Swede (formalistic and proper) writes, "Which Forms of Address to Use with an Elephant." The Dane (Epicurean and hedonistic) writes, "Ten Recipes for Elephant." The American writes, "How to Make the Elephant Bigger." The German writes, "Brief Preamble to the Introduction to the Love Life of the Elephant in Eight Volumes." The Norwegian writes, "Norway and We Norwegians."

Yet another flexible type of humor is the lightbulb joke, which points out the foibles of your group of choice. And my choice:

> How many Zionists does it take to change a lightbulb?
> Four. The first to make a donation for the purchase of the bulb. The second to convince the third to actually change the bulb. And the fourth to announce that the activity has the support of the entire Jewish people.

Honeymoon humor is also ubiquitous. But similar jokes can be quite different in tone and meaning, depending on the culture. Here's the non-Jewish version of such a story:

> A bridal couple checks into a hotel for their honeymoon. Just as they are about to make love, the bride is afflicted with the uncontrollable shakes of St. Vitus Dance. The groom calls the desk and asks that four bellboys be sent up. When they arrive, he says, "Okay, fellows, just hold her arms and legs, I'll do the rest."

Here's the Jewish version:

> A bridal couple checks into a hotel for their honeymoon. He is a yeshivah student and has spent most of his young life in study and prayer. So, when she prepares for lovemaking, he simply stands there.
> "What are you waiting for?" she asks.
> "I must tell you. I am completely inexperienced in such things," he replies.
> "Oh, there's really nothing to it," she says. "Take off all your clothes." He complies. "Now get into bed, and position yourself just so, above me."
> The groom complies and asks, "And now?"
> "And now," replies his bride, "daven!"

The basic facts are the same. The Jewish version is far gentler and less cruel. There is no element of force or indifference involved. And it is a quintessentially Jewish joke. The pivot is the word *daven*—prayer with a whole lot of shaking going on—by the groom, not the poor, afflicted bride of the non-Jewish version.

> The Dubner Maggid, the renowned Preacher of Dubnow, was invited to preach at synagogues all over eastern Europe. His wagon driver would take him from town to town, where the Maggid would give his stirring and learned droshe[2] at the Friday service. After which, he would be the honored guest at a great banquet, sitting at the dais with the town elders while the poor wagon driver was relegated to the backbench.
> One day, the driver tells the Maggid, "You know, just once, I would like to taste the pleasure of being honored as you are. I think, after all this time, I can give your droshe. They don't know you in the next town. Why don't we just change places?" The Dubner Maggid, always one for a joke, quickly agrees.
> They come to the town with the Maggid driving and the driver, dressed in the Maggid's robes, in back. The Jews welcome the apparent Maggid and invite him to the synagogue, where he gives the standard droshe brilliantly! If anything, he does it even better than the Maggid himself. The townspeople are beside themselves with admiration.
> At the banquet, while the driver is partaking of the delicacies at the dais, the town elders, carrying a volume of the Talmud, approach him.
> "Rebbe," they ask, pointing to a particular passage, "we've been studying this passage all week and do not understand it. Can you please explain it?"

---

2. Homily

The driver peers at the text, scratches his head, tugs on his beard, and finally announces, "What do you mean you can't understand it? This passage is so simple, even my driver could explain it. Come on up here, driver, and show them!"

This tale had made the rounds of the professional physicists' community as "Einstein's chauffeur." And, of course, it works. But there is yet another variant of the tale, which adds a quite specific element of Jewish culture. In this version, the Rabbi of Chelm and his driver switch places. After the conclusion of the version above, the observation "the townspeople realized that not only was the Rabbi of Chelm a great scholar, but even the simplest of Chelmites was a finer scholar than most ordinary Jews" is added. This wry comment derives its irony from two sources: first, the obvious myth of Chelm as a town of fools, and, second, from the original tale of how Chelm came to be, which was discussed in Part One above. Just to remind you, an angel passed over Chelm with two sacks: one of wise souls and one of foolish souls. A wind came along and caused the angel to drop one of the sacks. Thus Chelm was formed. The question of whether apparent foolishness is actually hidden wisdom—and the reverse—is a staple of oral and written Jewish tradition. The Chelm variant of the joke plays nicely on this ambivalence.

By the way, there is also a story in which the Chelmites discover cooked meat when a barn with a cow in it burns down. So, whenever they want cooked meat, they burn down a barn. Could this be the source of Charles Lamb's "A Dissertation upon Roast Pig"? (You should pardon the expression.)

The following story of Russian Jews has found its way onto the e-mail circuit:

> The KGB gets an anonymous phone call. "Yankl Rabinowitz is hoarding diamonds in his firewood."
> The next day, KGB agents raid Yankl's home and chop up all the wood, but they find nothing.
> No sooner do they leave than Yankl's phone rings. "Hello, Yankl? This is your neighbor, Shimen. I saw the KGB was there. Now it's your turn. I need my vegetable patch plowed."

Cute story. But it goes back at least to World War II when American soldiers' mail was censored. So one GI writes home to his wife, "Whatever you do, don't plow up the north forty. That's where I've got the loot buried."

The next story, here showing the wisdom of the rabbi, appears in its non-Jewish form in many a mathematics puzzle book:

> A father dies and leaves his entire estate of seventeen cows to his three sons. The stipulation is that the eldest gets half the estate, the next gets a third, and the youngest gets one-ninth. The sons are completely confused about how to proceed, so they ask the rabbi. After some thought, he brings in his own cow. The herd now numbers eighteen. The eldest son gets nine, the middle son gets six, and the youngest gets two. That leaves one, which the rabbi takes back home.

And here's one with a Jewish version and a scientist version. The Jewish version:

> Three Russian Jews are riding in a train through the Polish countryside when they see a herd of cows with black-and-white spots outside the window.
> "From this, we may conclude," says the first, "that Polish cows have spots."
> "No," ventures the second, "we may only conclude that some Polish cows have spots."
> "Indeed not," opines the third. "We may at most conclude that some Polish cows have spots on one side of their body."

The scientist version:

> A mathematician, a physicist, and an astronomer are hiking. Upon reaching a grassy summit, they see a black sheep. The mathematician notes this is evidence at least one sheep that is black on at least one side exists. The physicist remarks that the probability of observing a black sheep in this area is greater than zero. The astronomer exclaims, "Eureka! All sheep are black!"

Note how the same story told in two different ways can make different points. The Jewish version parodies the one-upmanship that often characterized Jewish scholarship. The scientist version pits three stereotypes against each other: the mathematician's extreme caution and obsession with minutiae, the physicist's "Heisenberg Uncertainty" leading to vague probabilistic statements even in the face of clear evidence, and the astronomer's penchant for observing a small part of the sky and extrapolating to the entire universe.

> An old couple comes to a lawyer.
> "We want a divorce."
> "A divorce? How old are you?"

"We're both ninety-five. And we've hated each other for decades."
"So why now?" asks the lawyer.
"We wanted to wait until the children died."

An old Jewish couple comes to the rabbi.
"We want a divorce."
"A divorce? How old are you?"
"We're both ninety-five. And we've hated each other for decades."
"So why now?" asks the rabbi.
"We just thought, shoyn genug!"³

A bit gentler indeed. The humor of the first version comes from its shock value. The Jewish version owes its humor to the absurdity of patient resignation.

In late nineteenth-century Russia, in the midst of the pogroms, two Jews decide to assassinate the czar. They find out he passes a particular street corner every day at noon, so they conceal themselves nearby and wait. Noon comes. No czar. Twelve-fifteen. Twelve-thirty. At a quarter to one, one Jew turns to the other and says, "I hope nothing's happened to him."

The Irish tell the same story. Instead of the Jews, it's two Provisional IRA gunmen. And, instead of the czar, it's a member of the Royal Ulster Constabulary. Superficially, the joke is the same. However, there is a deeper irony in the Jewish version. The IRA and the RUC are well-matched adversaries. But two Jews and the czar?

Here's a story that came over the Web as a blonde joke. Aside from the tastelessness of blonde humor, it completely misses the point. And it will be obvious why. Here's the Jewish original. Indeed, it is specifically American Jewish:

A Jew decides to convert to Christianity. He goes to a priest, who says, "I'll be glad to convert you, providing you can satisfy me that you know the basics of our faith."
"Ask away," says the Jew.
"What is the meaning of Easter?"
The Jew quickly replies, "Jesus was crucified on Good Friday and buried in a cave. On Easter Sunday, he arose from his tomb and went out among the multitudes."

---

3. Enough already! (You forgot it from the Katmandu Lama joke?)

"Excellent," says the priest, "and then what did he do?"
"He looked around, he didn't see his shadow, he went back into the cave, and they had six more weeks of winter."

If you replace the Jew with a blonde, all you have is a dumb blonde joke. However, the point of the Jewish version is not that the Jew is dumb. That's not one of the stereotypes of Jews. Rather, the message, the quintessentially Jewish message, is, no matter how hard they try, Jews will always be tripped up in their attempts to become Christian.

And talking about the Web, here's an old Jewish joke that got recycled:

> One autumn, a Jew is shipwrecked and washes up on a desert island. There, he manages to survive by living in a cave and eating roots and berries.
> The next spring, just before Passover, he sees a lifeboat approaching the shore. In it is a lovely young woman. It turns out she has also been shipwrecked, and it turns out she is Jewish. He shows her his island. She looks at the cave and says, "I think we can do better than this." Without further ado, she pulls an axe out of her knapsack and proceeds to chop down some saplings. From which, she fashions a lovely wooden house.
> She sees his store of roots and berries and remarks, "Let's see what we can do about that." She explores the terrain and collects a host of exotic fruits, vegetables, and grains, which he didn't know were edible.
> She asks what he's had to drink all this time.
> "Water."
> "I think we can do better." She constructs a still. While she is preparing a sumptuous dinner from the collected foods, the still produces a delicious alcoholic fruit beverage.
> At the conclusion of the dinner, she gazes into his eyes and murmurs, "Isn't there something else you've been missing that I can provide you?"
> He looks back at her excitedly and cries, "You brought matzoh?"

A recycled version, with no ethnicity specified, has the punch line, "You brought e-mail?"

Finally, one Russians tell about Chechnya and one's wife, but also told by Chicago Jews, about ... well, you'll see.

> A Russian finds an old-fashioned oil lamp. He picks it up and rubs it. Out comes a cloud of smoke, which materializes into a genie.

"You have released me from the lamp," says the genie, "so I must grant you a wish."

"Total victory in Chechnya."

The genie reaches into the folds of its ectoplasm and pulls out a map of the area.

"That's a pretty tough wish. Look at these mountains. Guerrillas can hide anywhere. And they have the support of the population. Listen, haven't you got an alternate wish?"

"Yes," says the Russian, "make my wife beautiful."

The genie is silent for a minute and then replies, "Maybe we better have another look at that map."

Eh, not such a good joke. Nasty, and not very funny. Now here's the Jewish version:

A Chicago Jew is walking along Lake Michigan when he spies an old-fashioned oil lamp. He picks it up and rubs it. Out comes a cloud of smoke, which materializes into a genie.

"You have released me from the lamp," says the genie, "so I must grant you a wish."

What does a good Jew wish for?

"A full and secure peace in the Middle East."

The genie reaches into the folds of its ectoplasm and pulls out a map of the area.

"That's a pretty tough wish. Look, here's Lebanon with Hezbollah supported by Iran. Syria sits on the Golan Heights. Not to mention Hamas in Gaza and Jewish settlements scattered around the West Bank. And then there's Jerusalem. Listen, haven't you got an alternate wish?"

What does any Chicagoan wish for?

"The Cubs should win the World Series."

The genie is silent for a minute and then replies, "Maybe we better have another look at that map."

Finally, here's one I've only heard with Jewish characters, but I think it would work for any other ethnic group:

Six retired guys are playing poker in their Miami Beach condo rec room. Goldstein loses $500 trying to fill an inside straight. He clutches his chest, staggers, and falls to the floor ... dead.

The question is: How are they going to tell Mrs. Goldstein?

Mandelbaum says, "Don't worry. I can do it diplomatically."

He goes to the Goldstein apartment and knocks. Mrs. Goldstein comes to the door.

"I've got some bad news," says Mandelbaum. "Your husband just lost $500 in poker and is afraid of how you might react."

"Tell him he should only drop dead!" she replies.

"Okay," says Mandelbaum, "I'll tell him."

CHUTZPAH

"Chutzpah," reads the Merriam-Webster Online Dictionary, is "supreme self-confidence; nerve, gall; temerity." And that doesn't say the half of it. The reason the word has come into English and has achieved such popularity is because it expresses a level of boldness hitherto unknown in the Anglo-Saxon world.

So what exactly is chutzpah? Well, it's like a Supreme Court justice's description of obscenity. It's hard to define, but you know it when you see it.

> A Jew presents himself at the gates of Heaven in 168 BCE at the height of the Maccabee revolt.[1]
> "Before we can admit you, we need evidence of your virtue on the earth," says the Angel of Judgment.
> "Well," says the Jew, "I was a soldier in the Maccabean Army and fought for a free Jewish commonwealth."
> "Did you commit any notable acts of courage?" asks the angel.
> "I believe so," replies the Jew, "I was captured by the enemy and brought before Antiochus, their king. He asked me what I had to say for myself, and I replied, 'You and your army are a bunch of barbarians, not fit to live with pigs, and we shall defeat you and drive you back into the caves where you belong!'"
> "Wow," exclaims the angel, "when did you say all this?"
> "About three minutes ago."

Swedish Jews tell the story of their ancestor, the first Jew allowed to immigrate to Scandinavia, in the seventeenth century.

> He is met at the shore by the king of Sweden, who tells him, "I will grant you anything you need to practice your faith."
> The Jew replies, "Nine more Jews."[2]

---

1. Whose successful conclusion we celebrate on Chanukah
2. Ten Jews are needed to make up a *minyan*, the minimum contingent for communal prayer.

Here's a story Galitsianers tell about their legendary folk hero, Hershele Ostropolier:

> The wealthy Brodsky says to Hershele, "If you can demonstrate chutzpah without thinking, I'll give you a ruble."
> Hershele shoots back, "One ruble? You promised me two."

French Jews tell a similar story about the Jewish writer Tristan Bernard:

> Baron Rothschild says to Bernard, "I hear you're funny. Make me laugh."
> Bernard replies, "I hear you're rich. Give me a million francs."

> President Clinton is visiting New York City during his 1996 reelection campaign when he suddenly gets hungry at 10:00 AM. He asks his entourage to stop at the nearest eatery, which turns out to be Sam's Deli in Brooklyn. They go in, and Clinton orders a pastrami sandwich.
> Sam is beside himself with delight. "Mr. President, this is such an honor. I voted for you, and now here you are in my restaurant. I'm only sorry about one thing. It's so early that the place is empty. No one will believe me if I tell them I met you. I only wish you could come back at lunch hour."
> "That's not a problem," says Clinton. "I'm in New York the whole day, and I'll sure be hungry again about noon. How about if I come back then?"
> "Oh, Mr. President, it would be such an honor," says Sam.
> At twelve sharp, Clinton returns. Sam's Deli is packed. Clinton walks up to the proprietor, puts his arm around him, and says, "Howdy, Sam!"
> Sam looks up at the president and says in a loud voice, "Bill, please, can't you see I'm busy?"

> The prime minister of Israel is visiting the United States. The president wants to make him a gift of a new Buick.
> "I'm sorry," says the prime minister, "I'm not allowed to accept a gift from a foreign government. But it would be okay if you sold it to me."
> "All right," says the president, "I'll sell it to you for five dollars."
> "It's a deal," says the prime minister. He reaches into his wallet and pulls out a ten-dollar bill. "That's all I have."
> The president looks in his wallet and says, "Sorry, but I don't have change."
> "That's okay," says the prime minister. "Just give me two Buicks."

> An Israeli is walking down the street in Jerusalem, chuckling. He stops the first passerby and says, "I heard a great joke about our dumb prime minister, and I've just got to tell it to someone."

The passerby replies, "I am the prime minister."
"Okay," says the Israeli, "I'll talk slow."

In occupied France during World War II, a beautiful young woman, an old woman, a Frenchman, a German officer, and a Jew are sitting in a train compartment. As the train passes through a tunnel and the lights go out, there is heard the sound of a kiss. The sound of a slap follows. When the lights come back on, the German is holding his cheek. What happened?
The German thinks the Frenchman kissed the young woman, and she slapped him (the German) by mistake.
The old woman thinks the German kissed the young woman, who then slapped him.
The young woman thinks the Frenchman kissed the old woman, and she slapped the German by mistake.
The Frenchman thinks the German kissed the young woman, and she slapped him.
In fact, the Jew kissed his own hand and then slapped the German.

Cohen is picked up by the Gestapo in occupied Copenhagen and brought to their headquarters at the Dagmar Biograf [3] for questioning. As he sits in the commandant's office trembling with fear, the phone rings. The commandant picks it up, listens for a minute disgustedly, hands the phone to Cohen, and tells him, "I don't speak Danish. You translate."
Cohen takes the receiver and says, "Gestapo. Cohen speaking."

Berl and Shmerl decide to share in the construction of a common succah.[4] Berl will build it, and Shmerl will pay for the materials.
When the construction is finished, Shmerl refuses to pay. Berl takes him before the rabbi. The rabbi listens to the story and rules, indeed, Shmerl doesn't have to pay.
"By what reasoning?" asks the anguished Berl.
"The Talmud," says the rabbi, "tells us to consider the succah as if it was our house. And, as is well known, Shmerl never pays his rent."

"Mr. Friedman," asks the IRS auditor, "how is it that you have deducted four trips from Chicago to Israel as business expenses for your delicatessen?"
"We deliver."

---

3. Cinema (Danish)
4. Hut of branches and leaves Jews build each year to celebrate Sukkoth, the Feast of Tabernacles, the week after Yom Kippur

Poor Mendl Katz is diagnosed with mental illness and is placed in a nursing home. Once there, he demands kosher food. The home complies, at considerable expense.

One Friday night after dinner, the director passes by Mendl's room and smells smoke. He walks in to find Mendl puffing contentedly away on a Havana cigar.

"Mr. Katz," says the director, "you demanded kosher food, yet you are smoking on your Sabbath, which I know is forbidden. How do you explain this?"

"Simple," says Mendl, "I'm meshuge."

OUT-OF-THIS-WORLD HUMOR

Oddly enough, American Jews have created a humor based on encounters of Jews with aliens—*real* aliens. Why is this so? Is it simply because, when Jews say, "Our humor is universal," we really mean it? Well, part of Jewish humor is meant to reflect the universality of the Jewish condition. Part of it derives from the common Jewish encounter with alien societies. Extraterrestrial Jewish humor is based on the absurdity of carrying these ideas to their extremes.

> A Martian lands on Earth and encounters its first Earthling. The human asks, "Where are you from?"
> "Mars."
> "Do all Martians have three arms?"
> "Yes."
> "And five legs?"
> "Yes."
> "And two tentacles for eye stalks?"
> "Yes, we do."
> "And do all Martians have such sad eyes?"
> "No," replies the Martian. "Just the Jews."

> A Martian spacecraft crashes on Earth, and one of its wheels is broken. The Martian goes looking for a replacement. He (She? It?) chances upon a delicatessen with a display of bagels in the window. The Martian goes into the deli and asks, "Can I have one of those wheels for my spaceship?"
> "Those aren't wheels," says Moe the counterman. "Those are bagels."
> "What do you do with them?" asks the Martian.
> "We eat 'em," says Moe. "Wanna try one?"
> "Sure." The Martian takes a bite, chews, reflects for a minute, and opines, "You know, this would go good with cream cheese and lox."

> The first spaceship lands on Mars. The three astronauts disembark, look around, and hear a whirring, chattering noise in the distance. They follow

the sound and eventually come upon a flat plain. Sitting in the middle, working away on sewing machines, are two Jewish tailors.
"Who are you?" says one of the tailors.
"We're astronauts from Earth."
The tailor looks at his partner. "We need pressers, and they send us astronauts."

The first Israeli astronaut lands on Mars, and immediately radios back, "There is evidence of life here. I have found a feather."
"What kind of feather?" Mission Control radios back.
The astronaut radios a reply, "What am I, a milliner?"

Two Martians meet. "What's your name?" asks one.
"Z3X94W," answers the other. "And yours?"
"Y7Q48K."
"That's funny," says Z3X94W. "You don't look Jewish."

THE FUTURE?

So much for space travel. I think it would be fitting to end this book with a little time travel—into the future. Jews always worry about continuity. Will there be a Jewish people in the future? Or will we all just assimilate and disappear? This final story nicely tweaks both Jewish assimilation and the Jewish obsession about it.

> The year is 2060 CE. Two Jewish women meet on the street. The first is pushing a baby carriage with two infants, a boy and a girl.
> "Mazel tov," says the other. "When were they born?"
> "Six weeks ago."
> "And what are their names?"
> "The girl is Brokhe and the boy is Shloymeh. They're named after their great-grandparents, Brittany and Scott."

GLOSSARY

In cases in which the popular spelling has been used in lieu of the standard YIVO orthography, the popular form is listed, followed by the YIVO form in parentheses. An *e* at the end of a word is pronounced as *eh*.

Apikoyres: Heretic
Ashkenazim: European Jews
Azoy: Like this
BCE: Before the Common Era. Used in lieu of the Christian BC. See CE.
Balagole: Wagon driver. Pronounced bah-la-GOH-leh.
Baleboste: Woman of the house. Pronounced bah-leh-BOS-teh. Also connotes a highly competent woman.
Bar/Bat mitzvah: Confirmation service for thirteen-year-old males/females
Biz hundert tsvantsik: (May you live) to 120
Bris: Circumcision, performed eight days after birth. *Bris* literally means "covenant," denoting the contract between the Jews and God.
Brokhe: Blessing
CE: Common Era. Used in lieu of the Christian AD. See BCE.
Challah (Khale): Egg twist bread; eaten on the Sabbath
Chutzpah (Khutspe): Gall
Daven (Davn): Pray, but referring only to Jewish prayer. Generally accompanied by shaking and swaying.
Der Forverts: *The Forward.* This secular Jewish newspaper is published weekly. Today, it is referred to as *Der Forverts*, without translation, because there is an English-language Jewish newspaper called *The Forward.*
Galitsianer: A Jew from the Galicia region of southeastern Poland
Got: God
Goyim: Gentiles; plural of goy, Gentile.
Goyish: Gentile (adjective). Often refers to typically non-Jewish behaviors, such as hunting. Or eating pastrami on white bread with mayonnaise.
Goyisher kop: Gentile head
Ikh hob dir in drerd: Literally, "I have you in the earth." "Go to hell" is a good English approximation.

Haggadah (Hagode): Passover service book
Halakhah (Halokhe): Jewish law
Hassid (Khosed): A male follower of Hassidism, a branch of Judaism founded by Israel Baal Shem Tov in the eighteenth century. A female follower is a khside. Plural: khsidim and khsides, respectively.
Kaddish (Kadesh): Prayer for a dead parent or other loved one
Kapote: Long gabardine, caftan
Kashe: Buckwheat groats
Kheder (Kheyder): Elementary school for Jewish boys, starting at age three
Khnyuk: Religious fanatic
Kibbutz: Israeli communal farm
Kibbutznik: Member of the kibbutz
Knesset: Israeli Parliament
Kosher: In keeping with Jewish law regarding food. Preparation of all food from farm to table must be supervised. See Mazhgiekh. Specific strictures include no meat and milk products eaten together. No shellfish. No pork. Definitely no bacon cheeseburgers.
Kotel: The Western Wall, the only remaining wall of the Jewish Temple in Jerusalem, destroyed by the Romans in 70 CE. Commonly referred to (but not by Jews) as the Wailing Wall.
Koved: Honor
Kreplekh: Dumplings. Like wontons, except not filled with pork.
Litvaks: Lithuanian Jews
Mamzer: Bastard
Matzoh (Matze): Unleavened bread; eaten throughout Passover to commemorate the tradition that the Jews fleeing Egypt had no time to let their bread rise. Matzoh comes in a cardboard box, which it resembles in taste and texture.
Mazel (Mazl): Luck
Mazel tov (Mazltov): Congratulations
Mazhgiekh: Supervisor of the food who ensures it is kosher
Melamed: Teacher of young children
Meshuge: Crazy
Mezuzah (Mezuze): A parchment with part of Deuteronomy, enclosed in a small case that is attached to the doorpost of Jewish homes
Mishnah (Mishne): The part of the Talmud that is a commentary on the Bible
Moyhel (Moyel): Ritual circumciser
Olev hasholem (Olevasholem): May he rest in peace

Ostjuden: East European Jews. German word used, often pejoratively, by German Jews. See Yeckes.
Oy gevald: Oh good grief
Oylem Habah (Habe): The World to Come; the afterlife
Pareve: Neither meat nor dairy; for example, vegetables or fish
Pesakh (Pesekh): Passover, springtime festival celebrating Moses having led the Jews out of slavery in Egypt
Peye(s): Earlock(s)
Reboyne-sheloylem: Master of the World (God)
Rosh Hashonah (Rosheshone): Jewish New Year; in the autumn
Sephardim: Jews from the Arab countries; originally from the Iberian Peninsula; expelled in the fifteenth century
Shabbes (Shabes): Sabbath
Shammes (Shames): Beadle, caretaker
Shatkhn: Matchmaker
Shayle: Question
Shikse: Gentile girl or woman; sometimes pejorative
Shiva (Shive): Seven-day mourning period
Shiva call: Condolence call
Sitting shiva: Observing the mourning period after the death of a relative
Shlep: Tote, carry
Shma: The fundamental credo of Jewish monotheism. It begins, "Shma yisroel adonoy eloheynu, adonoy ekhod (Hear O Israel, the Lord our God, the Lord is One)." "Barukh shem kvod malkhuso leyolam voed (Blessed is His glorious kingdom forever and ever)."
Shoyn genug: Enough already
Shul: Synagogue
Shtetl: East European Jewish village
Shtrayml: Fur hat worn by Hassidim
Siddur (Sider): Prayer book
Talles (Tales): Prayer shawl. The shawl contains a band with Hebrew writing at the collar and a series of elaborately knotted fringes at the ends.
Talleysim (Taleysim): Plural of talles
Talmud: The great codex of Jewish law; written and compiled in the first several hundred years CE.
Talmudic: Referring to the Talmud. "Talmudic" sometimes connotes hairsplitting, which Jews call pilpulistic and non-Jews call Jesuitical.

Tefillin (Tfiln): Phylacteries; boxes with Scriptural writings that observant Jews put on their head and left arm while reciting the morning prayers
Torah (Toyre): Literally, the first five books of the Bible and/or the scroll containing them. But it can also refer to the entire body of Jewish knowledge.
Treyf: Nonkosher
Tsores: Woes, troubles
Un: And
Yarmulke: Skullcap
Yeckes: German Jews; Yiddish slang, often pejorative, by East European Jews. See Ostjuden.
Yeshivah (Yeshive): Institution of higher Jewish learning
Yiddisher kop (Yidisher kop): Jewish head
Yinglish: Mixture of Yiddish and English; the only tongue my great-aunts and -uncles spoke fluently
Yom Kippur (Yonkiper): Day of Atonement; eight days after Rosh Hashonah
Yontev: Festive day; holiday
Yontevdik: Festive; holiday-like
Zloty: Polish coin

978-1-58348-628-3
1-58348-628-3

Made in the USA
Lexington, KY
29 March 2011